The Attack on Higher Education

Maurice Kogan with David Kogan

Kogan Page

First published in Great Britain in 1983 by Kogan Page Ltd,
120 Pentonville Road, London N1 9JN

British Library Cataloguing in Publication Data
Kogan, Maurice
   The attack on higher education.
   1. higher education and state – Great
   Britain   2. Education, Higher – Great
   Britain – Finance
   I. Title   II. Kogan, David
   378.41   LC178.G7

   ISBN 0 85038 755 8 (Hb)
   ISBN 0 85038 756 6 (Pb)

Printed and bound in Great Britain by
Billing & Sons Ltd, Worcester

Contents

Abbreviations

ABRC	Advisory Board on Research Councils
APR	Age Participation Rate
ARC	Agricultural Research Council
AUT	Association of University Teachers
CFE	College of Further Education
CNAA	Council for National Academic Awards
CVCP	Committee of Vice-Chancellors and Principals
DES	Department of Education and Science
MRC	Medical Research Council
NAB	National Advisory Body for Local Authority Higher Education
NERC	Natural Environment Research Council
SERC	Science and Engineering Research Council
SSRC	Social Science Research Council
THES	*Times Higher Education Supplement*
UCCA	Universities Central Council for Admissions
UGC	University Grants Committee

Foreword

Most of the material in this book comes from printed and public records. Our debt to particular sources, and notably the *Times Higher Education Supplement*, will be obvious from the text. The other principal sources are the proceedings of the Education, Science and Arts Committee of the House of Commons, which vigorously questioned the government's actions throughout the period in which the cuts were being imposed.

Some of the leading figures in politics and education gave us valuable interviews. Even those whose views we criticise were helpful and courteous in meeting us and discussing these events. Among those whom we interviewed were: Professor John Ashworth, John Bevan, Mark Carlisle, MP, Lord Flowers, Sir Alec Merrison, Sir Edward Parkes, Christopher Price, MP, Laurie Sapper, Sir Morris Sugden and Dr R W J Keay (secretaries of the Royal Society), the Hon William Waldegrave, MP and Phillip Whitehead, MP. The AUT allowed us access to valuable data on the impact of the cuts. We are in debt to the Inner London Education Authority, and particularly to Christine Mabey, who helped us to contact schools and colleges in inner London and advised us (though the responsibility remains ours) on formulating the questionnaire which is reported in Chapter 10. We express our thanks to the 40 or so schools and colleges who replied to our inquiries.

Our thanks to others must also be recorded. Tony Becher, Piers Burnett, Godfrey Golzen, Mary Henkel, Raymond McAleese and Peter Scott read and criticised our text. Sally Harris was an expert transcriber of tapes of interviews and of successive drafts of this book. Our publisher, Philip Kogan, was all that a publisher should be, both encouraging and demanding. Stephen Moss's editing puts the reader – as well as the authors – in his debt.

Maurice and David Kogan
June 1983

1. The Attack on Higher Education

In 1981, the government launched an unprecedented attack on higher education in Great Britain. Although ministers have been ignorant of the implications of their policies, it is now certain that between 1981-82 and 1984-85, when the number of 18-year-olds seeking places in higher education will be at a peak, 18,000* undergraduate and graduate home and EEC places in the universities will be lost. This is in addition to the 5,300 places held by overseas students which were lost between 1979-80 and 1982-83.[1]

Some 5,600 academic and academic-related posts will be disestablished in the universities in the next two years, and a similar number of non-academic posts will disappear. Ten thousand academic and related posts will be lost in the whole of higher education, of which 6,000 will occur through early retirement.[2] The universities faced great costs in getting rid of staff, and initially had no promise of help in compensating those induced to leave.

These cuts are the results of a policy that was carelessly created and is being unfeelingly administered. Four months after the government had announced its cuts in March 1981 it still did not know how many student places would be lost as a result. A year later, William Waldegrave told the House of Commons that as many as 61,000 young people who would have gained places in previous years would fail to do so between 1982-83 and 1984-85.[3] Yet in April 1983, the government published figures demonstrating that the reduction in potential candidates between now and the 1990s would be far less than had been assumed in 1979. As a result there would not be enough places available for qualified and willing students. Each step was thus taken by the government in ignorance of its consequences.

What are the motives underlying the policy? One version, persistently stated by a junior minister responsible for higher education, William Waldegrave, was that the policy had no ideological intent,

---

*Or 23,000 if the universities' peak year, 1980-81, is taken as the base. Some universities had failed to follow the University Grants Committee's 'advice' to restrain undergraduate admissions in the previous year.

and was derived simply from the need to cut public expenditure. The policy is thus 'expenditure led'. But this argument runs counter to those of Waldegrave's immediate predecessor, Dr Rhodes Boyson, who maintained that cutting higher education would have positive benefits. Moreover, although the government had little notion of the consequences and costs of its actions, its policy, begun in ignorance and confusion, gathered particular biases as it developed. It exploited the confusion created by the cuts to insinuate changes in the purposes and running of higher education. It shifted the line between universities and polytechnics, changed the basis on which overseas students are financed and introduced its own, employment-related, preferences into the staffing of universities.

The government made its cuts first by increasing overseas student fees, thus withdrawing, haphazardly, important financial support from particular institutions. It blithely assumed that universities would continue to recruit the same number of students, despite the increase in fees, and so would not need the same support from public funds. In 1981 the government administered a further 8.5 per cent cut, which cumulatively meant a cut of 13 per cent within three years. The universities had already lost 10 per cent of their income per student in the 1970s. These changes came into effect just as the number of 18-year-olds able to seek higher education was reaching its peak, and when, because of deepening recession and unemployment, more older people should have been encouraged to take up full- and part-time places.

After it had cut the universities, the government found that it could not control entry to higher education courses provided by local authority institutions, although it drastically reduced the central 'pool' of money available to them. Nor could it stop local education authorities, which control the majority of these institutions, from making good from the rates that income lost by cuts in the advanced further education pool. Nor did it have the power to stop local authorities from performing their statutory duty to give student awards to all who secured places in advanced courses. As a result, it had to seek parliamentary approval of supplementary estimates of £36 million for 1982-83 and £49 million for 1983-84.[4]

The universities were cut drastically at a time when the government had no policy for, and no clear grasp of what it had power to do in, the parallel public sector of higher education – the polytechnics and CFEs. Some 250 university courses were to be lost, whilst less good courses in institutions also supported by public money were to be retained. Students have been pushed over the 'binary' line dividing universities and polytechnics. And the polytechnics have been allowed to fill up and take on the students lost by the universities. The polytechnics, which in 1984 will be subjected to rationalisation by the newly created National Advisory Body, have actually increased their student numbers. The universities have been able to preserve some measure of financial superiority, while young people gaining a point or so less in A levels will go into overcrowded classes in the polytechnics.

Having made decisions about the universities, the government did not work out the detailed consequences, but left them to the academics on the University Grants Committee who, though opposed to the cuts in general, set about too loyally administering them.

In implementing the policy the UGC made a key decision to try to preserve the staffing ratios enjoyed by universities so that research would not suffer, while insisting that the number of student places be reduced. This decision may not have offended some university academics who, while believing it important to preserve access for able young people, also cherished existing standards of scholarship and research. As a result of the UGC decision, which was fervently endorsed by ministers, universities have had to turn away students or be fined by the UGC.* The extra tuition fees earned by taking higher numbers have been deducted from the grants to those universities who have refused to toe the line.

The UGC imposed the cuts in such a way as to reduce student numbers at a time when the number of 18-year-olds was reaching its peak. The UGC did so to preserve what it considered to be excellence, and particularly certain kinds of excellence in science and technology. It also selected the universities to endure the worst cuts on assumptions and through procedures that reveal particular kinds of academic bias.

If the cuts began simply as an attempt to save money they soon gave way to an open season for the exercise of political fantasy. Sir Keith Joseph pursued an obsession with the social sciences, forcing their budget down, inaugurating an inquiry into ill-founded allegations about the Social Science Research Council and compelling it to change its name. He devoted a great deal of energy to attempts to convert higher education into part of the market economy. The New

---

* As this book goes to press, it has been announced that this policy is to be withdrawn.

University of Ulster was compulsorily combined with a polytechnic because it was too small. Yet the tiny, private University College of Buckingham was admitted to the privileges of other universities, just as well-established universities lost 18,000 places. Just before the General Election was called there were press reports that Joseph was contemplating handing out a 'pot of gold' to an experimental group of universities.[5] They could admit as many students as they liked, at what fees they chose, and would pay student maintenance grants at what rate they chose. They would also have command over their own capital assets.

The universities and colleges have hitherto remained remarkably free of ideological pressures from politicians. It is curious to see Sir Keith Joseph compelling them to join him in a kind of monetarist's play school in which he can indulge his ideological fantasies.

If cost cutting was the objective, ministers went about it in a curiously uninformed and haphazard way. Ministers were not in a position to assess the likely savings, because they did not know the costs of breaking tenures nor did they realise how many disappointed candidates for university places would flood into the polytechnics and take up student awards. The government might have deliberately averted its gaze from the consequences of its actions. But can a government not hold itself responsible for caring, or even knowing, how many students will enter higher education?

Does it matter that universities have been cut and higher education so radically attacked? It could be argued that at a time when millions are unemployed the fate of 61,000 young people – and many more in the future – and of higher education teachers put into early retirement is not a matter for general concern. But it does matter. The satisfaction of individual demand for higher education as a means of achieving one's full potential is a citizen's right. Moreover, Britain is largely a country of the sub-educated; the vast majority of its citizens  left school at 14 or 15 and the proportion going on to higher education is small by the standards of any other developed country. The low level of education is one of the principal causes of the UK's economic and political problems. The failure to provide maximum opportunity for the young and for under-educated older citizens is both the symptom and the cause of a society's failures.

It matters when the policy is placed into the context of educational change since the 1939-45 war. One of the authors writes from the viewpoint of a higher education teacher who belonged to the post-war generation which benefited from the expansion of higher education.

The differences in opportunity created after the 1944 Education Act are strikingly exemplified in our own family. Not one member of it – sister, brothers, aunts or uncles – who reached the age of 18 before 1945 entered college or university. But the great majority of those of us – brothers, nieces and nephews – who reached the age of 16 after 1945 entered a higher education course of one kind or another.

To the vast majority of people brought up in the 1920s or 1930s higher education was an unattainable dream. Perhaps 80 per cent of each age group left school at 14, and those who stayed on until 16 were likely to use their school certificates to enter white collar occupations or craft or technician training. Less than one in 30 could hope to obtain a university place, and many of the universities themselves were small and short of money.

The turning point was the 1944 Education Act, which instituted local authority awards for university students, and made it possible for the less affluent to take up places at university. Higher education was seen as the path to success and personal fulfilment: a better job; a higher income; more leisure; and an opportunity for individual expression. These were the dreams entertained by many whose adolescence had been abruptly ended by service in the war. Those who grew up in the 1940s wanted to get on with their own lives, and saw university education as a great opportunity for personal development.

In the next three decades the terms of reference of higher education became wider: to provide opportunities for those who wanted to return later in life; to offer opportunity for those who could only take courses part-time; to help local industry and the community overcome specific problems of education and training. It was catering not just for a narrow elite, but for all those with suitable qualifications who could benefit from higher education. The touchstone was not only excellence but also development, and it was accepted that it is not the ablest who are the most worthwhile students, but those who travel the furthest distance from the lowest starting point.

Britain made astonishing strides to help more young people to fulfil their educational dreams. In 1945 only 3 per cent of each age group entered university. In autumn 1982 over 13 per cent of 18-year-olds entered full-time higher education. The number of part-time students, including mature students, has also increased dramatically. Almost 500 institutions in Britain now provide different types of higher education. These institutions range from long-established universities to locally based colleges which provide a wide range of courses at all levels.

In the early 1970s Mrs Thatcher, then Secretary of State for Education, argued in favour of increasing the numbers in higher education, and forecast that the proportion of each age group reaching higher education would approach 22 per cent. The system was expanded to make it possible to begin to reach this target. But in cutting higher education a decade later her government has not only reduced opportunity, but has also severely damaged several institutions.

This book therefore follows several themes: it is not the story of a clear-minded government pursuing a simple policy. Rather it is a story of how a decision to jettison 20 years of uncompleted educational development led to the uncovering of unstated motives and the emergence of unintended consequences. We show how the universities were damaged and humiliated in a way that was certain to reduce their teaching and research effectiveness. We show the impact of the policy on individual institutions and on academic tenure, and the effects on this generation of young people as they seek places in higher education. We raise the question of how the leaders of the academic system responded to the government's onslaughts, and the extent to which some were preconditioned to it, whilst a very few connived at the changes. We hold up to particular scrutiny the actions of the University Grants Committee as it went about implementing the government's policy. It was both less objective and less consultative than its spokesmen claimed. Leading academics too easily persuaded themselves that it was their duty to uphold criteria which would protect research at the expense of opportunity for the young, and divert reduced funds from the less to the better established institutions.

We also tell the astonishing story of how the government, having failed to restrict entry to the public sector (that is, all of higher education except for the universities and some voluntary colleges), both cut its funds and let it recruit the students whom the universities were now forbidden to take. The universities could now be thought of as providing for a narrower elite of students, while other types of students could be herded into an increasingly overcrowded and under-resourced public sector. The removal of easy access for foreign students, through the raising of fees to full cost, enabled ministers to make way for granting aid to students from their favoured countries. As the humanities and social sciences were culled, together with some of the less fashionable varieties of technology, so the universities and colleges could be allowed to scramble for money for the government's favoured subjects, such as information technology.

The government was careless in its planning and hypocritical in disassociating itself from the detailed consequences of its policy. The results will be profound and socially disastrous: a generation of young people lost to higher education; some thousands of prematurely retired academics who could be teaching those students now deprived of places; impairment of the country's scientific capacity, a point pressed on the government by both the vice-chancellors and the Royal Society; and the destruction of the liberal academic objectives set by the Robbins Committee in 1963 and adopted by the Conservative government of the time.

References

1. UGC Report on Reshaping Universities, DES press notice, 304/82, 22 December 1982
2. Answer by Dr Rhodes Boyson to parliamentary question, 6 July 1981, *Hansard*, HMSO
3. Answer by William Waldegrave to parliamentary question, 16 March 1982, *Hansard*, HMSO
4. DES estimates, 1983-84, p 10, class X vote, students' awards, etc, para 6, HMSO 1983
5. Auriol Stevens and Robin McVie, the *Observer*, 15 May 1983 and *THES*, 20 May 1983

2. The Expansion of Opportunity

> The government considers higher education valuable for its
> contribution to the personal development of those who pursue it; at
> the same time they value its continued expansion as an investment in
> the nation's human talent.
> (*Education: A Framework for Expansion*, government White
> Paper, 1972)

Between 1945 and 1970 the British higher education system virtually quadrupled in size. Immediately after the 1939-45 war a small group of institutions catered for an elite as much social as intellectual; in 1946 there were only 50,000 university students, but in the next 25 years the number and types of institutions, students and courses steadily increased. Although the University Grants Committee expressed anxiety that such an expansion would erode academic standards, the number of full-time students increased to 83,000 by 1948-49, and further expansion proved irresistible as a larger number of young people qualified for entry.

The post-Robbins consensus

The reasons for this expansion in the '50s and '60s were economic and social, but it was possible because both major parties accepted the need for it. A Conservative minister, R A Butler, piloted through the 1944 Education Act, which increased opportunity at all levels of education. Subsequent Tory ministers, such as David Eccles and Edward Boyle, followed Butler's lead by recognising the need for a wider system of entry to higher education, and by 1963 there were 216,000 full-time students. In 1963 Sir Alec Douglas Home's Conservative government accepted Robbins' radical proposals for further expansion. The Robbins' Committee report represents a landmark in policy-making, and reflects the confidence and expansionist thinking of the period. It recommended an increase of nearly 350,000 places in higher education between 1963 and 1981, and proposed that the proportion of each age group going on to higher education be raised from 8 per cent to 17 per cent.

Expansion of the higher education sector was also encouraged by the build-up of pressure from the schools as each year more young people stayed on to obtain qualifications which made them eligible for entry to college. The UGC report for 1961 remarked on this 'trend', which was accentuated by the 'bulge' caused by the increase in birth rate immediately after the war. It was against this background of burgeoning qualified demand that the 1963 Robbins Committee stated that 'courses of higher education should be available for all those who are qualified by ability and attainment to pursue them and who wish to do so.' [1]

This was the principle of social demand. It made it legitimate for expansion to continue as long as increased demand for places was sustained. The Robbins Committee and governments of both parties accepted the principle without qualification. They did not contemplate a restriction of opportunities if economic difficulties arose, nor did they accept the argument that expansion would dilute standards, that 'more will mean worse'.

The principle of opportunity for suitably qualified school-leavers was sacrosanct: any well-motivated candidate who secured a minimum of two Es at A level should, it was maintained, be able to find a place in higher education. The same policy was implied by the Conservative government's acceptance of the 1962 Anderson Committee's report, which led to legislation making it compulsory for local education authorities to give grants to all full-time students entering higher education courses demanding two or more A level passes. Both major parties accepted that higher education was a prime consumer good, which rewarded merit and improved society.

Higher education was thought to be good both for individuals and for the country. Politicians treated it with kindness and deference. In 1971 Edward Boyle explained why Home's government had accepted the Robbins Report almost immediately after publication.[2] The government, Boyle said, had a bad conscience both about its quarrel with the UGC in 1962 over the level of grants made to universities and about its treatment of university pay. It felt it must compensate for a decision which was a 'bad one and a hard one to defend'. Boyle also recalled that the first debate he had to answer at the Conservative Party conference in October 1962 was a debate calling for the expansion of higher education.

Later the Labour Secretary of State for Education, Anthony Crosland, who had no particular sentiment about the universities and who greatly preferred to promote the cause of the newly designated polytechnics, acted with great delicacy in bringing the universities under the eye and claw of public audit. Although universities' books were to be open to the officers of the Comptroller and Auditor-General, they would accept the accounts certificated by the universities' own auditors. This quite mild demonstration of the rules of public accountability provoked a massive (and still fascinating) report by the Public Accounts Committee, which records both the fears of academics that their freedom would be infringed and the insistence of the government officials that this would not be the case.[3]

Even at the beginning of the 1970s belief in higher education as an undisputed good was sustained. Speaking in 1971 Edward Boyle said: 'Now that voices, usually hailing from All Souls, or wherever, are saying that Robbins was a great mistake, and that this concentration on the numbers of qualified students was, and is, a great mistake, it is worth recalling the pressure there was in the 1960s to expand higher education.' Boyle was prepared to support Robbins' assertion that 'there was a great deal of potential ability still there, if we were willing to help it'. 'I would have thought', said Boyle, 'that the norm of opinion by 1965 was clearly on Robbins' side.' There seemed to be a remarkably strong consensus that higher education should continue to expand as long as young people were prepared to qualify to enter it.

Despite this all-party acceptance of the need for expansion there were challenges to higher education as it grew. One attack was contained in *A Black Paper: Fight for Education*, edited by C B Cox and A Dyson, which for all of its exhortations about academic standards is undated but probably published in 1969.[4] It complained that the teacher 'is no longer regarded as the exponent of the great achievements of past civilisation . . . politicians and even vice-chancellors have been imitating the fashion, and there is great danger that the traditional high standards of English education are being overthrown. In the universities, students are claiming the right to control syllabuses, to abolish examinations, and even to become involved in appointing their own teachers.' This document, produced by a Conservative pressure group, contains a stream of complaints about radical student thuggery, the appalling consequences of expanding the London School of Economics, occurrences at Berkeley in California, and the break-up of the community of scholars.

The growth of higher education was also being questioned from other, less sceptical quarters. By 1969, Shirley Williams, the Labour minister of state responsible for higher education and generally assumed to be sympathetic to it, was pressing the universities to reform themselves. She offered an agenda of 13 points for reform, all of which implied that the universities' tradition of academic excellence must now be tempered by the need for greater economy.

In a speech in 1982 William Waldegrave, the minister then responsible for higher education, argued that Mrs Williams' warning had been blindly ignored by the universities.[5] Williams had hoped that the universities would cut their unit costs – the amount of money allowed for each student place – in order to increase the numbers and widen the range of students enjoying higher education. To do so, as Waldegrave was not slow to point out, she was prepared to reduce or even remove student grant aid by introducing a system of loans, to reduce the admission of overseas students, and to accept higher student/staffing ratios.

The 'binary' system

The creation of the binary system – the addition of a second layer in higher education led by some 30 polytechnics in England and Wales and central institutions in Scotland – greatly increased the range of educational opportunities. This second layer now comprises over 400 institutions offering a wide range of post A level courses. The 1960s were a period of radical change in higher education, and, though we may not agree with the creation of the binary system and the artificial divide it produced, it was a striking achievement to establish a new sector of higher education.

The Council for National Academic Awards became the validating body enabling non-university institutions to provide degrees of a reputable standard. Robbins had assumed that more institutions would offer degree courses. The report suggested that most institutions would eventually qualify for admission to the university system, that teacher training institutions would become parts of universities, and that only 12 per cent of higher education would remain outside the universities.

Anthony Crosland's variation of Robbins was the binary policy, which deliberately set about to create a separate, but equal, system. In a speech at Woolwich Polytechnic on 27 April 1965 he maintained that there was an ever-increasing need and demand for vocational, professional and industrially based courses that could not be fully met by the universities. He argued that these courses and the institutions which provided them should not be placed on a ladder leading to university status, or there would always be a residual public sector which would become a permanent poor relation, 'perpetually deprived of its brightest ornaments, with a permanently and openly inferior status'. It was important that a substantial part of higher education should be 'under social control' and 'directly responsive to social needs', and he wanted local government to maintain a reasonable stake in higher education.

Crosland argued that 30 polytechnics in England and Wales and the central institutions in Scotland should lead the public sector in higher education. They would take part-time students who wished to follow higher-level courses. At the same time, the public institutions would sustain their links with 'lower' forms of further education and with the local community. By 1970 197,000 students were taking advanced courses in the further education sector, and 28,000 of them were taking degree courses. By 1982 there were almost 2,000 courses leading to CNAA-validated degrees being taken by over 150,000 students in 151 institutions.[6]

The establishment of the binary system was not the only achievement of the 1964-70 Labour government. It also laid the foundation for the Open University. The OU could only recruit students over the age of 21, but could vary traditional entry qualifications. It immediately increased the number of adult students in higher education by nearly 20,000, and by 1980 there were 60,000 OU students.

The 1972 White Paper

The expansionist policy of the Wilson government reflected the political consensus favouring growth in higher education. This policy was continued by Margaret Thatcher, who, as Secretary of State for Education and Science in the Heath government, was able in a 1972 White Paper, *Education: A Framework for Expansion*, to announce a policy that would continue to expand higher education.[7] She looked forward to providing by about 1981 'for something of the order of 200,000 entrants annually from within Great Britain aged under 21. This would represent about 22 per cent of the age group then aged 18, compared with 7 per cent in 1961 and 15 per cent in 1971.' The White Paper went on to say that: 'The government considers that needs would be met within a total of 750,000 full-time and sandwich higher education places in 1981. This figure has accordingly been adopted as the basis for the government's longer-term planning in higher education.' The number of full-time and sandwich students in higher education in 1971-72 was only 463,000, so the White Paper envisaged an enormous and continuing increase in places.

Mrs Thatcher affirmed her faith not only in increasing student numbers and therefore in spending more money, but also in liberal values:

> Opportunities for higher education are not . . . to be determined primarily by reference to broad estimates of the country's future needs for highly qualified people; although attempts to relate supply to likely demand in certain specialised professions . . . will be no less important than before. The government consider higher education valuable for its contribution to the personal development of those who pursue it; at the same time they value its continued expansion as an investment in the nation's human talent in a time of rapid social change and technological development.

Perhaps a hint of future rigours can be detected in the words that followed:

> If these economic personal and social aims are to be realised, within the limits of available resources and competing priorities, both the purposes and the nature of higher education, in all its diversity, must be critically and realistically examined . . . The government hope that those who contemplate entering higher education . . . will the more carefully examine their motives and their requirements; and be sure that they form their judgement on a realistic assessment of its usefulness to their interests and career intentions.

Despite this warning shot the White Paper makes 1972 feel like the Indian summer of British education. It stood as one of the latest in a long line of liberal Conservative measures designed to increase opportunity for young people in higher education. From Butler to Eccles to Boyle to Thatcher the Conservative Party could claim an expansionist record in education – certainly one as good as that of the Labour Party. Yet within 10 years another Conservative government was to turn its back on policies of wider opportunity, and Mrs Thatcher's ministers were to move against the universities first.

References

1. Higher Education: Report of the Committee appointed by the Prime Minister under the Chairmanship of Lord Robbins, 1961-63, Cmnd 2154, para 31, HMSO 1963
2. Edward Boyle in M Kogan, *The Politics of Education*, p 93, Penguin 1971
3. Special Report of the Committee of Public Accounts: Parliament and Control of University Expenditure, session 1966-67, 290, HMSO 1967

4. C B Cox and A Dyson, A Black Paper: Fight for Education, Critical Quarterly Society, undated

5. Speech made by William Waldegrave, Westfield College, University of London, 17 November 1982

6. Toni Griffiths, 'The development of higher education since the Robbins' Report', Appendix E to *Excellence in Diversity* by Gareth Williams and Tessa Blackstone (in press)

7. *Education: A Framework for Expansion*, Cmnd 5174, para 118, HMSO 1972

3. Uncertainty Grows (1972-80)

The 1972 White Paper was the last government pronouncement from which higher education institutions could derive any reasonable certainty about their future size and levels of support. From then until 1979 they were subjected to a series of stops and starts in which forward planning became impossible and the greatly cherished quinquennial* system of grants to universities fell into abeyance. One vice-chancellor, Stephen Bragg of Brunel University, quoted Dorothy L Sayers in complaining to the UGC in 1973 that its latest directive was 'like the thirteenth stroke of a grandfather clock which sheds doubt on all those which precede it'.

Expansion falters
In stating that there were to be 750,000 higher education places (22 per cent of the age group) by 1981, Margaret Thatcher had already reduced the figure of 835,000 which was the DES target in 1970.[1] Thereafter, forecasts were steadily revised downwards. In 1974, the 1981 target was to be 650,000. In 1976, it was reduced to 600,000, and it was admitted that this would mean more competition for entry in some places. In 1977 it was reduced to 560,000 and places were distributed between the universities (310,000 places) and the other higher education institutions (250,000 places). This reduction in planned numbers was accompanied by a falling-off of recruitment.

The number of 18-year-olds leaving school with two A levels rose steadily, but the percentage seeking and going to higher education fell. It peaked in 1972 at 14.2 per cent but six years later was down to 12.4 per cent. In part this reduction reflected the fact that teacher training courses ceased to accept students with fewer than two A level passes.**

---

* Under this system universities received advance notification of their grant for a five-year period.
** The DES now claims that since the higher age participation rate (APR) of the early 1970s included students in teacher training who would not be part of the APR of the late 1970s, the APR is now 'the highest ever', if an appropriate adjustment is made (DES Report on Education, No 99, April 1983).

All of this made it easy progressively to weaken the arrangements for making grants to universities. Their grants were reassessed from 1975 onwards and fixed within a 'cash limit'. This was reduction by stealth, because inflation was allowed to erode their real value. By failing to account for inflation the UGC grant was reduced by 4 per cent for each student in 1976. Even then, the vice-chancellor of Cambridge University was warning that some university departments might have to close because of cash difficulties. Conservative politicians used the fact that such closures did not materialise to argue that the later and more justified protests of universities were equally without foundation. By the time that the Thatcher government imposed cuts in 1981, a cut of 10 per cent for each student had already been imposed and further cuts in income resulted from the imposition of full cost overseas student fees.

This was a period of growing uncertainty across the whole range of private and public employment. Britain was entering a serious recession, and the extent to which higher education is different from, or a more deserving case than, industry or the social services is debatable. Higher education has never had any clear market criterion to justify its expansion. Yet arguments for expanding rather than contracting higher education during a period of recession had been made by at least one OECD visiting party. It pointed out how post-school training and education could be used to offset cyclical unemployment by improving the general level of education and offering retraining as the job market changed.

Hesitations in policy affected the administration of higher education. While government is entitled to enforce its assumptions about how much higher education there should be, particular problems are created if reductions are enforced over short periods. Higher education institutions need long lead times. A university or polytechnic recruits students in one year and they leave as graduates four or even five years after they are offered a place. Commitments of expenditure to research can rarely extend over less than a three-year period. Most institutions need between two and three years between contemplating a substantial change in the curriculum or in course structure and beginning its implementation. It has to be approved within the institution, announced to prospective students in good time for them to make their choices and, in the case of public institutions, go through the processes of validation approved by the Council for National Academic Awards.

The Oakes Brown Paper (1978)

The policy vacuum continued until in February 1978 Gordon Oakes, the Labour minister responsible for higher education, produced a consultative document called *Higher Education into the 1990s*, which offered alternative future plans for discussion.[2] This was the first attempt at rational planning based on consultation. It attempted to examine the likely impact of the falling birth rate on the demand for higher education. It set out low, central and high projections for the intake of various categories of students.

The Oakes projections were influenced by a document called *Population and the Social Services*, published a year before by the Central Policy Review Staff, which pointed out that, with a falling birth rate, the demand for higher education was bound to fall.[3] This would be so even if the proportion of young people entering higher education – the 'age participation rate' – continued to increase. The CPRS assumed the APRs adopted in the 1976 Expenditure White Paper: 14 per cent in 1977, 15 per cent in 1981-82, 18 per cent in 1990-91 and 19 per cent in 1995-96. Even given these increases, it concluded, 'this rise in participation rates would be insufficient to compensate for the fall in numbers in the relevant age groups after the mid-1980s peak.' To use all of the spare capacity would require an age participation rate of 22 per cent in 1995-96. By contrast, the proportion of the population over 75 and 85 would increase over the next 25 years and put increased pressure on the health, housing and personal social services. Thus the case for diversion of funds from higher education to other services was being formed.

The Oakes document contained two sets of calculations. It presented three different estimated age participation rates and offered five policy options. The three demographic or participation options were that the proportion of 18-year-old entrants might increase from 13 per cent in 1978 to 15 per cent, 18.3 per cent or 21 per cent in 1994-95. If 15 per cent was the chosen option, the number of full-time and sandwich students would increase from 520,000 in 1978 to 560,000 in 1981 and 600,000 by 1984-85, stabilise for about six years, and then go down to 560,000 in 1992 and 530,000 in 1994. The system would thus have to take some 80,000 extra students for six years and then suffer a contraction of 70,000 between 1990 and 1994.

The paper then set out five models for accommodating these demographic projections, one of which (model E) envisaged continued expansion after the mid-1980s by taking more working-class, mature and part-time students. A year later, however, government plans for student numbers for the mid-1980s virtually abandoned the expansionist model E variant.

This was at least an attempt to plan a system on well-defined premises. The Oakes document was also, like Shirley Williams' 13 points and Margaret Thatcher's 1972 White Paper, based on the Robbins principle. None of these documents argued for cutting higher education for reasons of cost. Oakes seemed to endorse the possibility of either increasing or sustaining the number of student places. He seemed to hope that more of the reduced numbers of 18-year-olds would want to enter higher education, and that many more under-educated people would enter an increasingly varied range of higher education courses later in life. As yet ministers and civil servants were not prepared to say, openly at least, that places for those qualified and wanting to enter higher education should be reduced in the interests of economy or academic 'excellence'. The Robbins principle was still intact, though being engineered to meet a new set of economic and demographic assumptions. And the issues were set out for debate in a way that the subsequent Conservative government never attempted.

Nobody reading the Oakes document can fail to be impressed by the terrifying complexities facing educational planners. There would be a peak of 941,000 18-year-olds in Great Britain in 1983. The number would fall to 630,000 in 1994-95, so there would be a 'hump' which could either be 'tunnelled through' – by allowing the APR to creep up from 14 to only 15 per cent – or, alternatively, higher education would be expanded at great cost to take the 1983 peak of the hump. This would allow for a higher participation rate to include many more mature, female and part-time students to fill the places left free by a reduction in the number of 18-year-olds between 1983 and 1994.*

---

*In the Brown Paper, model A assumed expansion and contraction in line with projected numbers. Buildings and staff would be acquired to cope with the hump, but would no longer be needed in the 1990s. Model B assumed reduction of expansion after 1981 to avoid damaging contraction after 1990. This would make it more difficult for school-leavers to enter higher education in the peak years and would abandon the Robbins principle. Model C was a 'resources' approach. The hump would be provided for, but on a basic budget. Buildings would be rented and staff employed on a temporary basis. A 7 per cent squeeze in buildings and staff/student ratios would result. Model D would encourage students to take two- rather than three-year courses or study part-time or defer their entry. Intake would thus be satisfied but the total number constrained. Model E assumed that there might be no decline in the number of students in the 1990s because of new recruitment patterns.

In the face of these proposals the academic system remained ambivalent. The universities, in particular, failed to grapple with the political problems that would soon face them. We would argue that they should have expanded their student numbers, even if this meant six or seven years of overwork until the 18-year-old age group subsided. The arguments against doing so were that, once universities showed they could operate on a poorer staffing ratio, they would never have been allowed to return to better standards, and that research would have suffered.

Higher education would not necessarily have been given an easy ride if Labour had remained in office in 1979. The Labour Party had been edgy, since the late 1960s, about the performance of higher education. It felt that it was too elitist and not prepared to change its ways to meet social needs, and its 1983 Election Manifesto made it plain that money would go only to those willing to change. The Conservatives were remarkably quiescent about higher education policy, but were certainly not, from 1972, advancing the claims of yet more expansion. The old political consensus – that higher education was an undisputed good to be protected in all circumstances – was gradually being eroded. The universities were criticised for failing to adapt to social and economic need and to make places available for a more varied range of students. The public sector of higher education was also criticised for so-called 'academic drift' – the tendency to ape the universities' academicism. Most of the criticisms were directed to producing greater diversity and more efficient administration, rather than to reducing the size of system. Policy was still bi-partisan, and higher education continued to enjoy the support of both those who saw it as an equaliser of opportunity and those who thought it enhanced the lives of those who were already relatively secure in their social position.

The Conservatives return to power

Higher education was already facing challenges when, in May 1979, the Conservatives swept back into power. All Conservative governments within living memory have come into office promising to roll back the boundaries of the state. All have espoused the cause of hard-pressed taxpayers, particularly those who earn their living in the private sector, against the ever-increasing demands of public expenditure programmes. All have said that they will reverse that trend. Mrs Thatcher's 1979 election manifesto was no exception: 'The balance of our society has been increasingly tilted in favour of the state . . . This election may be the last chance we have to reverse that process.' But only the 1979-83 Conservative government has really carried through its programme and been prepared to do so without heed to the practical effects of its actions. These unintended consequences had caused Mrs Thatcher's predecessors to modify their policies, but she would accept little compromise.

The 1979-83 government was also quite different from any of its predecessors in its attitude towards established institutions. No previous government had been so hostile to the civil service or so vigorous in reducings its size, self-esteem and self-confidence. In the past, Conservative practice implied a belief that certain institutions hold British society together. Thus the civil service, if unloved, was regarded as the custodian of continuity and of a kind of enlightened neutrality, which would hold a decent balance between the public good and the advancement of private causes.

The universities had from 1945 enjoyed a love affair with Whitehall and Westminster. They were seen as a glowing example of how government could both fund, and keep its hands off, institutions of proven worth, and were part of the fabric of the kind of society which many conservatives cherished. Here the young could learn to be both independent and yet dependable. Just as the officers of the Brigade of Guards, at public expense, could develop their own idiosyncrasies and their own corporate identities and yet be called up to guard the beaches at Dunkirk, so could the dignified precocities of Oxbridge collegiate life, or the massive eccentricities of distinguished professors of history or economics or physics at London or Manchester, be recognised as part of the rich tapestry of British life. Idiosyncrasy and freedom could be reconciled with the serious purpose of producing a rational and dignified working elite and of providing the scientific and intellectual base upon which so much of Britain's achievements had rested. The strand of 'liberal' opinion within the Conservative Party which accepted this has always been hostile to the extension of state activity, yet conscious of the need to support the fabric of public institutional life if society is to hold together as free, productive and civilised.

The composition of the 1979-83 government, whose actions were to make it one of the most radical in recent history, substantiates this point. Almost all were products of a very traditional type of higher education. The majority attended either Oxford or Cambridge. Mrs Thatcher herself is a perfect illustration of the opening up of opportunity, which gave members of the working class and petty bourgeoisie access to one of the best undergraduate educations in the world. Her first Secretary of State for Education, Mark Carlisle, was a graduate of the University of Manchester. His successor, Sir Keith Joseph, is a fellow of All Souls College, Oxford.

At least as much as any previous government its policies depended on groundwork done by academics. Its economic advisers, Terry Burns and Alan Walters, were straight from the academic world. Indeed, its economic policies, depending on the arguments of Milton Friedman, reinforce Keynes' dictum that 'practical men who believe themselves to be quite exempt from any intellectual influences are usually the slave of some defunct economist.'*

The universities were part of the fabric of British institutional life, and even in the 1960s, when they provided some of the British establishment's most strident and hostile critics, their role was not questioned. But the government elected in 1979 had little time for tradition or established institutions. Its 'new right' radicalism was deep-rooted and intense. It meant what it said when it proclaimed its intention to disengage from some areas where the state had been active. It would not concern itself with the detailed consequences of actions taken to reduce public expenditure and encourage private initiatives. It would not be at all uncomfortable in withdrawing a good deal of public support from universities and other areas of higher education, and assumed that the consequences of those actions would be worked out by those who were paid to administer the system.

The new government proceeded, within a period of 21 months, to deliver two hammer blows – in the shape of major financial cuts – to the universities. Similar money cuts were to be made in the public sector, although their detailed consequences developed unevenly and opportunistically.

Educational policy

On entering office, Mrs Thatcher appointed Mark Carlisle Secretary of State and Dr Rhodes Boyson, the former headmaster of a North London grammar school, reluctantly converted into a comprehensive, was appointed junior minister responsible for higher education. He was denied the post of minister responsible for schools because DES officials argued that his appointment would lead to an

---

*Keynes went on: 'Madmen in authority who hear voices in the air are distilling their frenzy from some academic scribbler of a few years back' (*General Theory*, 1936).

outcry among teachers. (Despite this Dr Boyson – a long-standing opponent of comprehensive education – did become junior minister for schools 18 months later.) Carlisle had no background in educational policy or practice and was generally regarded as being on the 'wet' side of the Conservative Party, while many thought that Boyson had too much knowledge of, and too many prejudices about, education.

This unlikely pair of wet and dry, innocence and experience, entered office with a general Conservative mandate to restrict public expenditure, but with no specific mandate on higher education policy, on which the Conservative election manifesto had said nothing. Conservative backbench opinion was ambivalent about cuts in higher education, but, in spite of apparent uncertainties in Conservative policy, the newly elected Thatcher government began, within weeks of entering office, drastically to reduce the scope of higher education. Sir Geoffrey Howe's first Budget in June 1979 cut large sums from the rate support grant, which enabled local authorities to finance public sector higher education. It also reduced university recurrent grants, student awards and medical school capital grants; cut polytechnic, college and university building programmes; and cut the budget for scientific research.

By August 1979 the UGC was already warning universities to reduce their intake of students next year by 6 per cent because new cuts could be anticipated in 1980-81. It was 'inevitable', wrote Edward Parkes, chairman of the UGC, that the target of 308,000 university students in 1981-82 would be reduced. Rhodes Boyson was already saying that intakes in some subjects must be reduced to allow others to expand.

In October 1979 the vice-chancellors were warned by the UGC that there would be no growth in real terms for universities for a number of years. It also announced that overseas students, whose fees accounted for 13 per cent of university income, would have to pay the full economic cost of their courses. Alec Merrison, the chairman of the Committee of Vice-Chancellors and Principals (CVCP), described these decisions as 'potentially disastrous'.

In November 1979 the Expenditure White Paper announced that education spending in 1980-81 would be £411 million less in real terms than in the current year. No specific figure was given for higher education, but the increase of overseas student fees to the full economic cost was confirmed. The universities were then asked to work out the implications of three options: no growth, a 5 per cent cut in their recurrent grant for the next year, and a 2 per cent rise in that grant.

The impact of these decisions was well documented by the *Times Higher Education Supplement* (16 November 1979):

> They [the universities] have been both stunned and confused by the Government's action; stunned by the nature, intensity and timing of the cuts, particularly in relation to overseas students, and confused because they still do not have hard figures or prospective student targets with which to work.
>
> As an example, university officials in the north-west had to call a hurried conference to see if they could agree what the UGC letter meant.

There was a flurry of senate, planning committee and other meetings. Nobody could know what proportion of overseas students would continue to come if the fees were to be increased as the government required. The LSE thought that it would lose between 10 and 15 per cent of its income in the first term and that student numbers would fall between 29 and 35 per cent over the next four years. Ralf Dahrendorf, its director, said that the general theme of the government's policies, on overseas students, immigration laws, cuts in the BBC, and its attitude to the EEC, indicated parochialism and a withdrawal from the world. 'Our students say the present fee is already beyond their means. We will have to look carefully at all applications. I say this with tears in my eyes; there will definitely be a lowering of standards. We will have to accept some people who have the money and not the quality.'

At Lancaster, staff and students agreed to hold a joint teach-in, and a sit-in in the senate chamber had the full co-operation of the acting vice-chancellor.

Academic leaders opposed the changes. Even a number of Conservative MPs were unhappy about the cuts. But Rhodes Boyson made a robust defence of the policy when interviewed by the *THES*.[4] He thought that the proposition that it was a good thing for a vastly increased proportion of young people to go on to further education was no longer the attitude of the public. He suggested that there was a great deal of difference between what the agitators say Robbins said and what he actually said. He did not believe that two A levels necessarily meant that young people were academically able. A period of consolidation, he said, would do no harm. 'All the dons I talk to privately – as against the pressure groups with vested interests in society – I find agree with me.'

33

These bizarre assertions conflicted with government statements. In January 1981, while the White Paper reducing higher education was being drafted, the DES replying to the Select Committee's report, *Funding and Organisation of Courses in Higher Education*, said: 'The improvement of the age participation rate generally is the long-term aim of the government, within the financial constraints.' At one time, a junior minister who so actively disassociated himself from stated government policy would be sent back to the backbenches. But perhaps Boyson was stating the policy and the DES reply to the select committee merely putting out smoke.

Boyson thought it to be the government's job to cut expenditure. Overseas students were costing £100 million a year.

All the groans have come from the university lobbies and not from the general populace. Two out of five overseas students are from Iran and Nigeria. We do not seem to have gained much advantage from Iran, nor from Nigeria, who nationalised our oil without paying for it. If that is investment it seems to be the worst we have ever made. The British universities are funded by the British rate-and taxpayer, not from outer space.

He thought that the outcry at the decision was just a 'knee-jerk of the left'. The universities were slightly hysterical about the possibility of failing to recruit enough foreign students. 'We will see what happens', he concluded.

Overseas student fees

The policy of increasing overseas student fees was the first direct attack on the universities, which had since 1976 been suffering the imposition of cash limits which made no allowance for inflation. The recruitment of overseas students had helped to offset the effects of stabilised home demand and to promote the liberal principle of open access. By attacking the universities' right to recruit overseas student fees at subsidised levels the government was not only reducing its 'subsidy' to overseas students, but also freeing itself of some of its obligations to maintain higher education places out of public money.

Successive small reductions in overseas student fees culminated in the decision in 1980 to start charging 'full cost fees' (some £2,000 a year for arts courses, £3,000 for science and engineering, and £5,000 for medical subjects). This decision ignored several important arguments in favour of continuing the subsidy: that additional students may create only marginal extra costs, that they helped to sustain demand at a time when home demand was flagging, and that overseas students tend to encourage contact (and trade) with foreign countries.

The effects of the policy differed from university to university. At some overseas student recruitment was down by 40 per cent in the autumn of 1980, but at another it was up by almost three-quarters. At the University of Manchester Institute of Science and Technology there was a drop of 20 per cent. The LSE was successful, after a sustained effort, in attracting large numbers of overseas students for newly marketed courses. London University suffered a drop of 5 per cent in overseas postgraduates and 4 per cent for all overseas graduates. The London Institute of Education was particularly badly hit, and new overseas admissions were down by more than a third. In 1980-81 there was an 11 per cent drop in the entry of students funded from overseas aid programmes, and in all 5,300 places were lost between 1979-80 and 1982-83. This was a significant decline, but constitutes a smaller drop than had been anticipated.

The number of students from poorer countries declined most, and many universities suffered as a result of the policy. Apart from the direct damage suffered to income, the haphazard nature of the effects again demonstrated the government's policy of acting first and considering the consequences later. Some of the best and most prestigious institutions had very large numbers of overseas students. These lost money with reference not to their needs but to the accidents of their previous recruitment.

The wider consequences of discouraging overseas students from attending British courses are likely to be serious. British universities lead the world in many academic disciplines, and many able scholars from overseas have received their undergraduate or graduate training in Britain. So, indeed, have many of the most distinguished leaders of British Commonwealth countries. Science and technology students from overseas have learned to respect British technology, and have become accustomed to using British scientific and technical equipment. These ties will now be damaged, and our academic and technical markets diminished. The government's decision – one made by little Englanders – disregarded Britain's role in the world of ideas, education and science.

Even government supporters now think the decision to end subsidised education for foreign students was an error. It created disruption: student leaders led sit-ins and other demonstrations which, while making little impact on government, destabilised college life at a time of great stress and falling morale.

The government came under pressure from various sources. In 1982 a report by the Outward Trust on the effects of the new policy helped to focus criticism and made proposals for a modest financial aid programme.[5] Foreign governments also protested, and by February 1983 the government had been forced into a partial change of policy. Fees remained at the newly inflated levels and no assistance was given to the universities hit hardest, but £43 million was put back by way of student aid on the Foreign Office Vote. These funds are given to students from countries of the government's choice, enabling the government to pursue its foreign policy preferences. Again, the pragmatic act of imposing economies had become a political weapon.

The policy contained a fallacy which was well stated by E G Edwards, former vice-chancellor of the University of Bradford. In an article in the *THES* he referred to the extraordinary notion that overseas students were being subsidised by an amount equal to the total cost of higher education divided by the total number of students. This, he said, ignored the fact that more than half of universities' costs can be fairly attributed to their research output. 'Yet the academic world, by and large, raised little protest at these curious economic fantasies put forward in their name. Is it possible that the oversight was due to an uneasy conscience?'[6]

References

1. DES Planning Paper No 2, 1970
2. DES, Higher Education into the 1990s, HMSO 1978
3. Population and the Social Services, Report by the Central Policy Review Staff, HMSO 1977
4. *THES*, Interview with Dr Rhodes Boyson, 'The doctor's prescription for cuts', 16 November 1979
5. Peter Williams (ed), *The Overseas Student Question: Studies for Policy*, Heinemann, for the Overseas Student Trust 1981
6. E G Edwards, 'Bleeding is no cure for this melancholy humour', *THES* 11 January 1980

4. Imposing the Cuts (1979-81)

The government's decisions to impose a policy of level funding and the end of subsidised student fees were followed by what the chairman of the UGC later described as a period of unprecedented dialogue about the future of the universities. This discussion gave the UGC information on which it acted when a further unexpected blow was delivered in the Expenditure White Paper of 1981. With the implementation of that policy, it was difficult to believe that the government was merely saving money wherever it could; whatever its statements of belief in the UGC's ability to create its own policy, it is inconceivable that ministers did not know that the expenditure cuts would lead to drastic cutting of the universities and unpredictable changes in the rest of the higher education sector.

Dramatis personae

Who was involved in these decisions? The Secretary of State who conveyed the decisions on overseas student fees and, almost as a last act of his office, the 1981 expenditure cuts, was Mark Carlisle. His period of office leaves no lasting memory except that of handing out Treasury medicine to the education system in as pleasant and moderate a style as possible. He is reputedly a 'wet', and is reported to have achieved the 'steady state' which followed the first series of cuts. But if he defended education he did so with remarkable lack of success in the long run. He, too, believed that the universities had cried wolf too often and that they could manage with less. Rhodes Boyson's views were even more clearly stated (see pages 33-4), and present a kind of ideological justification for what happened between 1979 and 1981 to higher education in Britain. (Confusingly, Boyson's successor has claimed there was no 'ideological' intent underlying government policy.)

If the Secretary of State who initiated the policies leaves no impression, neither does the permanent head of the DES, Sir James Hamilton. The constitutional convention is that permanent secretaries leave it to ministers to argue the merits of policy, but even by

37

this criterion Sir James Hamilton has been remarkably silent. Sir William Pile, his immediate predecessor, had not hesitated to state openly the DES's view that central government should play a greater role in the debate about the school curriculum. Sir Toby Weaver, a former deputy secretary responsible for higher education, had explicitly advanced and defended the policy of a binary higher education system. And DES officials had led the discussion on the Oakes Brown Paper.

We do not expect the leading civil servant to comment openly on government policy, but we would expect some evidence of concern with the consequences of such policies. The universities and polytechnics no longer felt they had any friends at court. Officials now seemed boxed in by ministers determined to impose cuts irrespective of logic or consequences. Cutting services and expenditure seemed to have become an irrefutable and higher truth incapable of logical critique or explanation.

The government left it to the UGC to put the policy into effect, and it was the UGC which took most of the blame for what happened. Its members, rightly, resent the assumption that the cuts were imposed by the UGC rather than the government. But the implementation of detailed policy rested with the UGC, and the criteria it adopted were wrong.

In September 1981 Mark Carlisle was succeeded by Sir Keith Joseph, Rhodes Boyson took over schools policy, and William Waldegrave assumed responsibility for higher education. Neither Joseph nor Waldegrave initiated the policy of cuts, but both vigorously pursued the policies laid down by their predecessors. Both, too, vigorously defended them before the select committee and through statements in Parliament and the press. Both are reputedly able men and fellows of All Souls, Oxford. Waldegrave is a moderate, whereas Keith Joseph is one of the sternest and most passionate advocates of hard-line monetarism.

Joseph's record in government has been that of a theorist of private enterprise who has not always succeeded in implementing his ideas. He thought money could be saved and higher education improved by chopping off parts of the public sector. But such a policy would be both difficult to implement – some colleges, for example, are owned by denominations – and unjust, because the public sector in education is designed to make higher education available to groups who would otherwise be denied access for personal or financial reasons. Joseph has argued for the privatisation of higher education, and has suggested that it should be partly self-financing and thus less dependent on the state. He has also argued for the conversion of the student grant system into one that will be at least partly dependent upon loans although that notion has recently been put in abeyance.

Both Joseph and Waldegrave lack experience in education. Joseph has had nothing to do with the public system of education, except as a minister presiding over its reduction. On his appointment Waldegrave was described by the *THES* as a 'high-flying, young, moderate MP'. He is a former member of the Association of University Teachers. He was a member of the staff of 10 Downing Street when Edward Heath was Prime Minister and head of Heath's office when he was leader of the opposition. He claims to have had close links with both the university and polytechnic in Bristol, where his constituency is.

Both the Carlisle-Boyson and Joseph-Waldegrave teams were composed of equal proportions of wet and dry conservatism. Carlisle, in imposing a series of cuts, was following Treasury instructions to save money rather than pursuing a vendetta against the universities. His department thought that the universities and higher education generally could be trimmed, and it is possible that some of the academics with whom he and Rhodes Boyson had contact conceded that 'rationalisation' was desirable. Rhodes Boyson provided some of the more extreme rhetoric to justify the cuts, but more important was the Treasury and DES reading of demographic trends and the fact that politicians and the civil service had abandoned the age participation rate targets established by Robbins in 1963 and Thatcher in 1972.

On entering office Joseph and Waldegrave were convinced of the case for cuts, but hopeful that a beneficial reconstruction of higher education would result.[1] Hence the somewhat feverish restoration of money over the next two years to advance certain favoured policy options: large sums for information technology; increased aid for overseas students from favoured countries; the 'new blood' policy; and the creation of the National Advisory Body for Local Authority Higher Education, which was set up to rationalise the public sector. Some of these changes of policy were opportunistic forays into the hitherto protected world of higher education to meet particular policy prejudices. Sir Keith Joseph is reputed to have fought hard to get compensation for those university teachers losing tenure; but the style of his letter to the vice-chancellor of Surrey University (see

Chapter 6), who led a deputation requesting more help to resolve redundancy problems, is very much that of the tough right-wing minister who wanted to see universities put their staff into the same market framework as anybody else.

Not only education ministers but other members of the government, too, seemed to think that it was open season in higher education. Thus Norman Tebbit, Secretary of State for Employment, declared in December 1982 that some universities would be demoted to the status of colleges of technology if they did not provide the kind of education which government thought most needed. In making this kind of statement, ministers have shown themselves curiously uncoordinated and even unconstitutional in their statements. To revoke a royal charter would be difficult and is certainly outside the legal and political competence of the Department of Employment. At one time, no minister would make a statement, let alone a provocative one of this kind, on a matter within the province of another.

If the DES hid behind the UGC in imposing socially damaging policies, the UGC co-opted itself to the state's policy of reduction. A central figure in this was Dr (now Sir) Edward Parkes. Dr Parkes is a distinguished engineer, who worked in industry, was a young professor at Leicester University and later at Cambridge, and vice-chancellor of City University before becoming chairman of the UGC in 1979. At City University he was, according to the *THES*, thought to be a liberal and democratic vice-chancellor. Those who know him as chairman of the UGC also testify to both his ability and reasonableness. But like many academics and academic leaders put under duress, he took a very narrow view of the purpose of higher education.

The University Grants Committee

The University Grants Committee has been thought of as a shining example of British administrative and political compromise. Various metaphors have been applied to it. Perhaps the least glamorous was that of a former chairman of the UGC, Sir John (later Lord) Wolfenden, who described it as a septic tank between the universities and government. It had been universally regarded, until the recent change in its fortunes, as a magnificently competent broker between the government, willing to dole out money to the universities for what it conceived to be good public purposes, and the universities, anxious to receive public money to pursue a mixture of private and public ends.

The UGC was established in 1919 by Treasury Minute, at a time when the universities were in serious trouble. Their student numbers had fallen, some buildings were crumbling, and they seemed unlikely to be able to survive without large injections of public money. Because it was thought that the universities would do their best work if left to their own academic devices, it was not the Board of Education but the Treasury which produced from under its own wing the University Grants Committee. Its chairman has always been a former vice-chancellor, or a former academic of distinction, and its members were originally drawn exclusively from the distinguished professoriate. More recently, ministers have appointed some members representative of industry, of the schools and of local authorities. The chairmen of the SERC and the SSRC attend meetings, as do assessors from the DES and, on occasion, other government departments. It has an infrastructure of 12 standing sub-committees covering different parts of the academic spectrum, and it can also create panels and *ad hoc* committees to undertake particular tasks.

The sub-committees are almost wholly recruited from academic practice. All of these appointments are made *sub rosa*. The members of the UGC are selected by the Secretary of State for Education on the advice of the chairman of the UGC. The chairmanship itself, which carries with it the rank of second permanent secretary has, in recent years, been subject to the approval of the Prime Minister, as well as the Secretary of State. (Harold Macmillan set the precedent that the Prime Minister should be involved in the appointment of all chairmen of public committees.) The members of sub-committees are, however, largely chosen by the chairman of the UGC, in consultation with the chairman of each sub-committee.

Although the UGC is formally independent of the DES its secretariat is wholly recruited from the DES. Until the most recent appointment in 1982, the secretary to the UGC was a deputy secretary from the DES. The post has now been downgraded to undersecretary. We should not make too much of what was presumably a manpower economy made at a time when quangos were being attacked and civil service numbers and gradings being reduced, but the downgrading of the secretaryship could reduce the effectiveness and independence of the official.

The post has traditionally been filled by highly regarded civil servants, for whom the secretaryship was an honourable peak in their career. This perhaps enabled them to feel a certain independence of the DES, since they were unlikely to have expectations of promotion to the very highest level of permanent secretary. But if the post remains at under-secretary level, apart from the symbolic importance of its downgrading in terms of the status accorded to universities, it may mean that the incumbent still has expectations of promotion and may be less willing to question the policies of the DES or its political masters. Members of the UGC have always had a warm regard for the ability and loyalties of their secretaries; their ability to remain wholly committed to the UGC may be impaired by this change.

The success of the UGC rested on the fact that it enabled public money to be put responsibly in the hands of academics who would then distribute it according to academic criteria. The framework decisions – how many student places, and the balance between research and teaching and undergraduate and graduate students – were determined by ministers.[1] But once those decisions were made, and finance for the cost of implementing policy agreed, academics could decide which institutions should get what and for which general academic purposes. Moreover, the UGC knew what sums were available five years in advance and could, therefore, tell universities what grants they would have over a whole quinquennium for such running costs as salaries of academic and non-academic staff. (This time-span is necessary to allow courses to be properly planned.) Larger building projects were subject to a separate capital building programme.

This system struck a good balance between decisions based on what society needed (embodied in the framework decisions made by government) and what academic excellence should be rewarded, in terms of the allocations made on the advice of the UGC to institutions. The relationship worked well within the context of relatively low inflation and steady economic growth, when government could feel comfortable with the commitments made five years ahead.

It also fitted a period in which policies were determined by the application of the Robbins principle; the main task was to estimate demand. But with the 1981 White Paper, the government decided there would no longer be an open commitment to providing for all who were qualified and willing to take places. The UGC was then compelled to act more in response to government preferences than academic criteria in its shaping of the university system. The relationship between institutions and the allocating bodies changes radically when expansion gives way to contraction. These moves were made overt in a letter from Sir Keith Joseph to the UGC in July 1982 in which he said it might be appropriate for ministers to take more explicit responsibility than previously for determining priorities affecting the broad character of allocations to universities.[2]

The UGC's role changed dramatically at the end of the 1970s, and even now its perception of its own role still remains confused. Dr Parkes made a vigorous defence of the UGC's decisions (*THES*, 17 December 1982) in which he said that the UGC was not an advocate for the universities. The UGC's job, as far as government is concerned, is to offer accurate analysis of the present, and, as far as it can, of the future. But it is surely naive to assume that a body consisting mainly of university academics will not put the universities' case to government. Nor is that role irreconcilable with proper analysis.

Dr Parkes also suggested that the UGC acts as a kind of consumer council for higher education. But the UGC is not a consumer council because it has executive powers. While in formal terms it advises the DES on the allocations made to institutions, those recommendations are, in fact, absolutely decisive. A consumer council, in all of the models of which we have knowledge in both the public and the private sectors, has no power to make executive decisions, or to advise on them, but takes up complaints on behalf of consumers. The UGC does not behave in that way. It receives framework decisions from government which it converts into executive action. Like all executive bodies it receives complaints. But that is very different from standing in the position of critic or watchdog.

The UGC must face two ways. It is expected to advise government on what should be provided for the universities and on the effects of policies, although those policies are for government to decide. While the Robbins principle of providing places for all who were willing and qualified to take them still applied, the UGC was mainly concerned with gauging the number of qualified students who could be recruited for the different undergraduate disciplines and the number of places necessary to provide for postgraduate study and research. (The government, however, retained control of the number of postgraduate home students through its allocations to research councils and other postgraduate funding bodies.)

The UGC had increasingly to compete with the public sector, but until the mid-1970s its main task was to calculate the case for more money, in the expectation that more students would or should be forthcoming. In its relationship with the universities, however, it took on an entirely different and non-advisory role. It allocates finance, on academic criteria, to different institutions, and by inference, to parts of institutions. It has enormous power. Within the allocations and policies made by government it is for the UGC to decide which university is worth backing and which is not. It was, for example, the UGC which decided which universities, of the 30 or so which wanted them, should have schools of law and which should not. Until the 1981 cuts it had rarely had to decide which universities and which disciplines to cut, but once government policy had moved in that direction it was plainly for the UGC to make such decisions.

Dialogue with the universities

On 15 October 1979 Dr Parkes wrote to the universities to record Mark Carlisle's achievement in cabinet: that 'on the committee's best judgement of the situation, it is probable that the total recurrent grant (subject to what has been decided on overseas students) will be held for a number of years at no higher level in real terms than that for 1979-80. If resources are not to increase there must be consideration of whether it is possible for student numbers to continue to increase.' Expansion had come to a halt, but was not yet put into reverse. The committee's 'best judgement' was to be demolished within 18 months. Edward Parkes thought that the 1980-81 entry and that of subsequent years must be reduced below that expected in 1979-80 if 'the roll-on effect of the entries of earlier years is not to produce a total population of undergraduate students substantially in excess of that expected in 1979-80.' In other words, 1979-80 was to be the peak year for recruitment and after that point the total numbers of students was to be held constant but not reduced.

Given this policy of level funding, and the cuts imposed through the increase in overseas student fees, the UGC invited the universities to predict the effects of applying a range of policies. It gave three possible future allocations for each university; by now they must have been used to playing with different hypothetical models. 'Hypothesis (b)' represented 'level funding' modified only in respect of the overseas student fees policy. 'Hypothesis (a)' represented a 2 per cent increase in grant. And 'hypothesis (c)' represented a 5 per cent reduction in grant.

During the first six months of 1980, the UGC met every institution on its grants list, as well as a number of schools of the University of London not on the list. This series of meetings was held amidst deepening gloom. The universities had already been compelled to charge full fees for overseas students. The three hypotheses would mean yet further cuts to be made on top of the effective 10 per cent reduction in the unit of resource – the amount of resources allowed for the teaching of each student – since 1976. Peter Scott, editor of the *THES*, wrote in November 1979 that this was the year in which the Robbins era finally ended.

From January 1980 the UGC held meetings with four universities a week, and vice-chancellors and a small group of their senior officers were cross-examined about the financial status and the proposed student numbers of their universities.

These discussions allowed the institutions to respond to a variety of proposed policies. The UGC later claimed that each discussion covered the institution's philosophy, its academic plans and priorities and the problems it faced. Edward Parkes told the select committee that these discussions were unique in the history of the UGC. 'Taken together, they provided the base for the whole of the committee's work over the subsequent 12 to 18 months and the material provided by each university, and the points which emerged in discussion influenced the committee's consideration of individual institutions at all stages of its deliberations.'[3]

Though this process has been hailed by the UGC as an unprecedented period of discussion with the institutions, many senior academics were hardly aware that it was happening. The discussions took place between vice-chancellors and the UGC, and entailed no detailed process of assessment of the departments and other components of the institutions; consultation within universities was variable. Yet it was upon these discussions that many key judgements were made which were later to determine policies. Discussions were held in London, and the officials of the UGC did not visit the universities. For example, the University of Stirling, badly affected by the cuts in 1981, gave evidence to the Education, Science and Arts Committee of the House of Commons on 29 March 1982 that it was not visited by the UGC between 1970 and 1982.

It may be that data can be acquired without visits, and both the UGC and other senior academics say that visits are not for the purpose of evaluating academic worth. But many academics would doubt whether a meeting with a vice-chancellor and selected members of his staff is a substitute for a full discussion about a university's role, particularly when the decisions being made are critical to the university's future. Universities are public assets. It is difficult to think of transactions of similar importance conducted with such privacy and with so little attempt at overt and comprehensive analysis of the relevant data. If this dialogue was as great a step forward as the UGC later claimed, it says little good about what preceded it.

Following these meetings, universities were invited to submit additional detailed academic information. In June 1980 they were asked for returns covering full-time home student numbers for 1979-80, forecasts of full-time student numbers in 1983-84 on the three hypotheses, and similar forecasts for part-time students. In November 1980 the UGC received detailed plans from the universities.

The 1981 White Paper

On 16 December 1980, the government abandoned its level funding policy and announced the reduction in funds for home students. The sheer waste of skilled manpower involved in requiring universities to generate these guesses on hypothetical grant levels while ministers were deciding grant levels of an entirely different order was considerable. Ministers must have cynically allowed the UGC to play these elaborate games with the universities at the very time that they were drafting drastically different prescriptions. In any event, the new policy was promulgated in the laconic terms of an Expenditure White Paper in March 1981:

> The reduction in planned expenditure on overseas students will result in a fall in total net current expenditure in higher and further education. Additionally, for home students in higher education the plans provide for a progressive reduction in expenditure so that by 1983-84 institutional expenditure (net of tuition fee income) will be rather more than 8 per cent below the level planned in Cmnd 7841. This is likely to oblige institutions to review the range and nature of their contribution to higher education. It is also likely to lead to some reduction in the number of students admitted to higher education with increased competition for places; but the government expect institutions to admit, as they have done this year, as many students as they can consistent with their academic judgement. The detailed implications of the plans for the university and non-university sectors are under discussion with the University Grants Committee and the local authority associations.

Taken together with the overseas student fees policies, these cuts seemed likely to produce a total cut in resources for universities of between 11 and 15 per cent in real terms between 1980-81 and 1983-84 (depending on the number of overseas students they could recruit); the actual figure turned out to be 13 per cent.

The universities were outraged. They had already felt seriously damaged by the previous year's policy of level funding, and the announcement of the 3.5 per cent cuts in 1981-82 in December 1980 was, they felt, already presenting them with almost insurmountable managerial problems. The chairman of the Committee of Vice-Chancellors and Principals (CVCP), Sir Alec Merrison, vice-chancellor of the University of Bristol, said that the vice-chancellors had not been given 'the slightest explanation for this quite extraordinary decision by the government'.[5] They believed the policy to be 'profoundly misguided'. They further believed that the White Paper's statement of intention to 'give protection to the support of basic science, an activity which underpinned further developments and . . . a particular strength of the United Kingdom, shallowly assumed that basic science could be protected when funding for the universities was being run down.' The vice-chancellors believed that the forced economies of recent years had already brought them to the end of the road of continuing their high achievement with reduced resources through more efficient management. The staffing ratio for universities, excluding medicine, was already 10:1 and must get worse, while that in polytechnics and colleges of higher education was 7.7:1. On this basis universities were hardly overmanned. 'For these reasons, we think it a kind of madness for the government at this particular point in British history to be planning a destructive onslaught on the universities.'

Merrison went on to complain on behalf of the vice-chancellors about the way in which the policy was being implemented. 'In the end the government can determine the level of activities in universities, because it controls our purse strings. But if it is their intention to reduce substantially that activity, then they are setting about it so clumsily as to guarantee the maximum amount of damage for a minimum of saving.' Savings could only be made through shedding staff. 'The time-scale imposed by government prevented this being undertaken through natural wastage. Savings could only be made by stopping recruitment and thus destroying the potential achievement of a generation of our most promising scientists and scholars.' The alternative would be to dismiss staff selectively. This would necessitate high redundancy payments.

At this stage, neither the vice-chancellors nor the government could be sure that breaking an academic tenure would not cost far more than the sums which were actually paid out in voluntary severances. The government was to stick obstinately to its time-scale – all reductions to be made within two years – because it feared the universities' ability to weaken the policies if they were given more time.

Merrison concluded his press statement:

THE ATTACK ON HIGHER EDUCATION

It must be the responsibility of the government to determine the size of the contribution universities will make to the nation's stock of highly qualified manpower and to basic and applied research. The government has already, quite contrary to the national interest, decided that that should be smaller. But the rate at which they want to run the universities down will inevitably ensure a drastic deterioration of the quality of what remains, which is even more important. We cannot believe that this policy has been arrived at with any kind of consideration of the social, economic or scientific consequences.

The UGC carries the ball

At each point, the UGC was required to work out the detailed implications of the government's decisions to reduce the income of universities sharply and without due notice. The UGC claims that it carefully assembled the data on which to base its decisions by holding discussions with the universities. Universities and colleges were, Parkes told the select committee, able to state their own strengths and weaknesses and to supply proposals on what they hoped to achieve given a variety of financial situations. When the most drastic cuts were introduced in 1981 the UGC began work with its sub-committees on the detailed decisions which it was to deliver in July 1981. It also consulted the research councils, such learned societies as the Royal Society and professional institutions, the CVCP, the AUT, the non-teaching unions and the National Union of Students.

What kind of data did the UGC use? In July 1981, when the storm had broken, Dr Parkes complained that there is 'a belief that the activities of the UGC are of a mysterious, secret and peculiar kind . . . they are merely somewhat complicated.'

As a result of its earlier exercises, the committee had statistics covering many key factors: demographic trends; the likely numbers of young people coming forward from the schools with particular levels of qualification; new entrants to universities; undergraduate and postgraduate student numbers; student attainments and first employment; and demand for short courses and part-time education. It also had data on university staff, finance and physical resources – buildings, laboratories, libraries, etc. More detailed tabulations were prepared as the UGC or its sub-committees required, including the number of applicants for places and the success rate for applicants. The UGC also thought it knew the attractiveness of different subjects to particular types of students, 'at least as measured in terms of their A level suitability and so on'.

48

There was a special inquiry on service teaching (ie teaching provided by one group of disciplines to others). The committee had details of research grants and studentships awarded by research councils, the DES, other government departments and other sources of research income; information on university reserves; and data covering special factors affecting mergers with colleges of education. But comparable data on the public sector of higher education were not available to the committee.

In March, when most offers of places are made, allocations began to be made for the academic year beginning in the autumn of 1981, and provisional figures were reached for 1982-83. The specialist sub-committees were invited to review the implications of reduced financing, and the committee itself considered the general implications for the size and operation of the system as a whole. Preliminary findings were then reviewed by the UGC in a series of meetings as information became available from the sub-committees and from studies of the system as a whole, and the implications for each institution emerged.

The committee considered various options: a reduction in the number of institutions; a 'tiered system' with a top tier liberally funded and staffed for substantial research, and the remainder financed primarily as teaching institutions; and the policy of equal misery for all. All were eventually rejected in favour of a selective distribution of student places within each subject group throughout the country, a policy which brought to an end the myth that the universities were free institutions able to determine how to spend money given to them by government.

The government had simply told the UGC to reduce expenditure on universities. It had given no lead at all on how the cuts should be administered. This is attested by both the chairman of the UGC and by successive ministers. Although it has been suggested that the DES influenced the UGC to save grants to students, the evidence shows that this was not the case. Once the UGC decided to make selective cuts among the departments representing subjects throughout the system it had to choose between allowing the unit of resource to fall or preserving student places.

Defence of 'excellence' led the UGC to argue that a further 10 per cent cut in the unit of resource, beyond the 10 per cent fall which had occurred since 1973-74, was the maximum that could be tolerated without attacking the research capability of the universities. So the UGC's package of cuts would contain a reduction in student numbers of about 5 per cent and a 10 per cent cut in resource levels for each student.

Whichever policy was adopted the sheer size of cuts in grants would have forced universities to reduce staff by some 15 per cent. The question then remained whether student recruitment or research would suffer most. Student recruitment lost.

This decision, more than any other, was made by academics rather than by Conservative ministers. The academics demonstrated their belief in sustaining certain levels of quality rather than in maintaining opportunities for young people to enter universities. The decision was made before the UGC or the government knew whether those young people would be allowed to find alternative places in the public sector of higher education – the polytechnics, colleges and institutes of higher education. In practice, many students who would otherwise have gone to university did find places lower in their scale of preference outside the university system. But the UGC was not to know that this would be possible, and did not know what cuts in the public sector might be on the way. It did know that many young people would be turned away from universities. As the UGC itself put it in a memorandum to the select committee: '*The outcome of the restriction on student numbers will be a deterioration in the overall participation rate of qualified and willing students from the present level of about 73 per cent to about 60 per cent until about 1990.*'[6]

Theoretically, the other 40 per cent could find places in polytechnics or other non-university higher education institutions. But, presumably, they would do so at the expense of their less well-qualified contemporaries, who would then fall out of the higher education system altogether.

Why did the UGC not advise government to close some universities? This would have accorded with the view of a few eminent academics that there were too many anyway. Closure would be traumatic for the individuals concerned, but at least other institutions would be able to continue with far less damage to their resources. But this was an inoperable policy. Generally speaking, the least favoured universities are the smallest. Both to close the least favoured and keep the appropriate balance between subjects would mean closing not just two or three but many more institutions before enough places had been cut. A reduction of 13 per cent of money in the whole system would mean taking out the whole of London University or, say, all of the places at Stirling, St Andrews, Heriot-Watt, Dundee and Brunel (other sacrificial names could easily be substituted). This would also distort the newly struck balance between arts, social studies and science, and to achieve the cuts, science and technology places would have to be transferred to other universities.

Having established its general principles, the UGC began to form judgements on each institution. It already had data from the earlier discussions. It now again considered its evidence on the demand for places, and the employment prospects of those who went to each institution. It located institutions within the national pattern of student places by subject. It considered such questions as the mix of students between undergraduates and postgraduates, home and overseas. It considered the age structure and grade structure of staffing in each subject. It contemplated the factors affecting the size of teaching groups. It considered evidence relating to the expensive subjects, such as medicine and veterinary studies, which required laboratories. It considered the evidence on unusual subjects and small departments. It also considered more subjective material on current research activity, the potential of each institution and the extent to which institutions enjoyed support from research councils and other funding bodies. The committee's view of the optimum contribution of each university to teaching and research within the system was adjusted in the light of successive examinations. The objective of the committee was 'to define and seek to establish an effective university system of a size which it would be feasible to maintain adequately at the level of resource planned by the government for 1983-84'.

The committee knew that the number and quality of students qualified and willing to enter science and technology had increased. It therefore decided that within the reduced number of student places available and because of the 'national economic interest', the proportion of students in physical sciences, technology, mathematics, computer science, business studies and some aspects of biology should be increased. In the UGC's own words:

> A heavy price had to be paid for this in terms of studies in other fields. This principally affected the arts and social studies, but it also affected medicine which had always been protected when the university system had come under pressure in previous times. As many as six student places in arts and social studies would have to be sacrificed in order to maintain one place in medicine; the equivalent costs of maintaining one science and technology place lay between two or three arts or social science students.[7]

51

Thus science and technology were sustained at the present level, but above-average reductions in arts and social studies were to take effect. In medicine, the target entry figure of 4,080 students was to be reduced to the actual 1980 recruitment level of about 3,850.

The UGC had reversed the policies it had pursued for eight years. In January 1973 it had expanded arts-based studies by 36 per cent at the expense of science and technology because, as it explained in its development plan sent to the universities, it was then bearing in mind the 'vocational demands in social and business studies and in medicine the projected demand for teachers of the social sciences in all sectors of higher education'.

The direct consequence of the government's reduction in funding and the UGC's determination to sustain the unit of resource was to deny a university education to a large number of young people, who would have received it had they been born one year earlier, or born in Sweden, the USA or West Germany, or in Finland, where in 1981-82 the higher education budget was increased by 23 per cent.

The letters to universities

On the basis of these judgements, student numbers and grant allocations were calculated. Grant letters to individual institutions were prepared, and these included guidance notes for each institution.

Letters from the UGC have always been regarded as of great importance to the universities. Before the quinquennial system was abandoned in 1973 the allocation letter was, in effect, the university's licence to develop and change in the certain knowledge that money would be forthcoming. Moreover, it was assumed that money would be augmented automatically to take account of unpredictable increases in salaries and other expenditure. Before the mid-1960s the UGC were very wary of telling universities what to do. Only in 1967 did they begin even to indicate the balance that might be struck between arts and science or graduate and undergraduate student places. From time to time they 'earmarked' grants to encourage particular developments in individual institutions, such as the growth of business studies. After 1967 UGC letters became more direct, but, even then, the universities retained a degree of independence.

The letters sent on 1 July 1981 (circular 10/81) were very different from anything received before. Their importance was signalled by the fact that they were placed in the library of the House of Commons. The University Grants Committee was now, for the first time in its history, telling every university in the country that it must 'substantially' or 'significantly' reduce student numbers in specific subject areas. And it not only went about systematically reducing courses such as Russian, which had not recruited sufficient students, but also required universities to make cuts in areas that were recruiting well.

These decisions were reached between the announcement of the expenditure cuts in the March White Paper and the issue of the letters to universities on 1 July. During this time, however, the full committee only met once a month. Despite this, the 'advice' was detailed. A typical example was of Aberdeen University which received the following 'advice' on particular subject areas:

> The committee recommends a reduction in student numbers in social studies and invites the university to consider discontinuing music... The committee recommends a substantial reduction in student numbers in the sciences, including the mathematical sciences. Within these reduced numbers it recommends that priority be given to the physical sciences and the committee invites the university to explore with the University of Dundee [a university many miles away] the academic and economic advantages of some co-operation in this subject area.

Aberdeen was also invited to discontinue Italian, and to explore with the University of Glasgow the possibility of deploying resources in Norwegian more economically. The UGC recommended an increase in numbers in biological sciences, and the maintenance of numbers in physical sciences and medicine.

The UGC, with its small staff and the enormous complications of the task set it, could not produce the letters on the promised day. Universities sent emissaries to 15 Park Crescent so that they could pick up their copies as they were released. They were immediately conveyed to their vice-chancellors and a process of textual decomposition then took place. It took some skill, for example, to comprehend that a 'significant' decrease meant a smaller decrease than a 'substantial' decrease. Some universities were eventually made privy to the fact that the UGC thought 'significant' meant more than 5 per cent and 'substantial' more than 10 per cent. Embarrassing mistakes were made. Non-existent departments were ordered out of existence. No university escaped unscathed. Even the most favoured in the latest and most draconian series of cuts had to accept a further 5 per cent cut in their grants. The worst hit of all lost 40 per cent.

References

1. House of Commons, Expenditure Committee, tenth report, session 75-76, Policy-making in the Department of Education and Science, memorandum submitted by the UGC, pp 324-32. This gives the best account of the respective roles of the DES and the UGC under the traditional arrangements
2. DES press notice 168/82 covering Sir Keith Joseph's letter to Dr Edward Parkes of 14 July 1982
3. Letter from Dr Edward Parkes to Christopher Price, MP, 2 November 1981
4. The Government's Expenditure Plans 1981-82 to 1983-84, Education and Science, Arts and Libraries, para 14, p 106
5. Committee of Vice-Chancellors and Principals, press information, The Funding of Universities: A statement by the Chairman, Sir Alec Merrison, 12 March 1981
6. Parkes to Price, op cit, para 9 (our emphasis)
7. Ibid, para 8

5. Responses to the Cuts

The universities were shaken by the letters sent by the UGC on 1 July 1981. They had, after all, responded to successive governments' demands to expand since 1945. They had felt assured, if decreasingly so, of the self-esteem that comes from being valued by a society which they believed they had faithfully served. Many of the country's ablest young men and women had not pursued the rewards of money or power that careers in business or the civil service might have brought them, in the expectation that they might undertake research and teach in freedom and security. Now the very existence of departments and the personal tenures of their academic staff were threatened by a government which cut first and worked out the consequences afterwards.

Reactions of the vice-chancellors

Three weeks after the letters were received, the Education, Science and Arts Committee of the House of Commons, and its chairman, Christopher Price, summoned both the Committee of Vice-Chancellors and Principals and the University Grants Committee to give evidence. Throughout this period the select committee applied constant pressure on the main protagonists to explain themselves.

Albert Sloman, the CVCP chairman and vice-chancellor of Essex University, criticised the government strongly in a letter sent in advance of the meeting.[1] The loss of income to the system, he wrote, would be something like 15 per cent by 1983-84, even when account was taken of the income recovered from fees charged to overseas students; that policy, it was now clear, would deprive universities of much of their previous income. 'The UGC', he said, 'has itself pointed out that losses of this order, over such a short period, can only produce disorder and diseconomy, however they are distributed between different institutions . . . Most universities will be severely damaged, some very seriously indeed.' There had been no attempt to sort out the relationship between the funding of universities and that of the public sector institutions. At a time of expansion competition might be healthy. But, Sloman continued:

At a time of contraction there can only be resentment if institutions feel that the cards were stacked against them simply because of the administrative category in which they happened to fall. It would be a matter of deep concern if departments were to be closed down in a university and their staff thrown out of work when no comparison has been made between their distinction and their productiveness and that of similar departments which are surviving in the public sector institutions.

While Dr Sloman thought that a university could be viable with less than 2,500 students, some universities might become bankrupt and have to close. He wanted the select committee to say that what was happening simply made no sense at all.

We are going to lose something like £500 million in income over the next two or three years. If what we have predicted comes true, the government will in the end have to put back something like half of that. [To pay for broken tenures.] To do what? To create chaos in the universities and to take away something like 20,000 places. It really makes no sense to do that. It would be much more sensible to allow that money to come into the universities so that they can run down the system more slowly.

The vice-chancellors were generous to the University Grants Committee. They still thought it to be the right body to make decisions between institutions. They wanted the widest possible discussion between the committee, with its national perspective, and individual institutions which were necessarily better informed about their own situations. The UGC had no option but to proceed at the pace imposed on it. In the past, however, there had been long periods of consultation. In this case, because the UGC had to move very fast: 'Consultation is now taking place . . . after the letters have arrived, not before they have arrived.' The vice-chancellors also hoped that the UGC would state its criteria more openly in future.

The UGC defends its decisions

The University Grants Committee, represented by its chairman and some of its members and secretariat, provided the select committee with papers on both the processes and the implications of the reductions over which it had presided. These, and other statements, implied that it had acquired sufficient information upon which to make decisions through the dialogues in the first half of 1980 with individual institutions, and later, with the different national representative and expert subject-based bodies.[2]

While he criticised some aspects of government policy, Dr Parkes implied that he did not think it appropriate for the UGC to address the issues of social policy which the government decision affected:

> The university system can function satisfactorily at any size that any government cares to name. What it cannot do is to change from one size to a smaller size at greater than a certain rate without a good deal of diseconomy occurring. The present rate of change is about twice the minimum rate at which you can do the job in an economic fashion.[3]

It was, it seemed, less the policy than the rate at which that policy was to be imposed that caused concern. A university could perform satisfactorily as long as academics could work within certain limits of size and financial constraints. But the criterion of which social purposes the universities might serve and for which social groups they might cater was ignored. Thus the UGC seemed more concerned with institutional well-being than with the social consequences of government actions, though it expressed some regret at the reduction of opportunity in its letter conveying the cuts to universities.

The UGC did its best to compel the government to face its obligations to meet the costs of making academic staff redundant. If it had not done so some universities would surely have gone bankrupt. It is reputed that Sir Keith Joseph, too, had to fight hard in the cabinet for a reasonable settlement. Dr Parkes had made a guess to the Public Accounts Committee of something like £150 million as the cost of a voluntary retirement scheme. Some £20 million had been allocated in 1981-82 for immediate redundancies, a figure plucked out of the air in the absence of guidance from the government. Much more would be required in 1982-83. The true costs turned out to be about £90-£100 million for academic and related staff and £30 million for non-academic staff.[4] There were additional costs in superannuation payments, as academics took early retirement.

These lower figures were achieved because a voluntary retirement scheme was agreed. Had universities attempted to enforce redundancies and had compensation been successfully contested in the courts, a figure nearer £250 million might have been reached. The first attempt at compulsion by the University of Aston was withdrawn at the end of 1982. The general adoption of the voluntary scheme led to the acceptance of far lower sums than the figure of £80,000 assumed by legal opinion to apply to a contested case. Again, however, money-saving ministers had no way of knowing that the cost would be as low as it turned out to be.

Dr Parkes told the select committee that the UGC had started to plan for a decline of resources for about 18 months, but it had not envisaged cuts as severe as those that were implemented. He was informed that the select committee had received anguished letters from universities up and down the country indicating that most felt that the assessment of quality had been 'highly superficial', that it had not taken account of end products and that it had not been moti-vated by the sort of balanced judgement 'that you have announced here to us'.

Parkes said that the UGC had not adopted regional criteria, though each university's contribution to the local community was considered. The UGC did not differentiate between the technologi-cal and non-technological institutions because, said Parkes, 'we had to treat universities generally as a single system'. He claimed that the UGC did not make arbitrary decisions. It had spent '18 months going round and round this trap'. The committee was concerned essentially with the national provision of resources, but this could conflict with what appeared to be the correct local priorities. He cited an example of this:

> Without naming the institution, for example, a particular vice-chancellor who has been to see me in the last few days has said to me 'Why on earth did you not tell us to close departments X and Y? Everybody knows they are appalling departments and we would like to get rid of them.' The answer to this question is quite simple; that there are weak subjects all over the country and we must maintain and hope to build them up.

The first reactions of the select committee were that the cuts would inhibit the development of continuing education, that the govern-ment should consider the comparative costs of maintaining a student against those of unemployment benefit, that the government ought to reassure universities on the issue of redundancy costs or slow down the reductions 'to remove the imminent risk of university bankruptcies', and that the government had placed the universities in crisis.[5]

It is part of the unfairness of the process that the government's decision to cut grants became virtually a background factor, almost an abstraction, whilst the decisions that fell to the UGC were made the target of the most searching criticisms and deepest resentments. The government skilfully hid beneath the skirts of the UGC. Its members had been co-opted to the allocative system to do justice between fellow academics, but now found themselves required either to resign and leave the dirty job to others who might do it worse, or, as some of its AUT critics implied, to act as agents of a government whose policy they disliked.

The impact on universities

The shock to the universities was enormous. The decisions arrived at the end of the academic year when university teachers had finished examining, and were preparing to go to conferences, or to write their books or articles or to do other research or just go on holiday. Many of them were involved in emergency senate and committee meetings and endless 'phone conversations. They had to draft papers and face difficult decisions. Should they seek to impose compulsory severances on their own colleagues, many of whom they had helped to select and appoint for tenure until the age of 65? If so, what criteria should be adopted? Should they send away their most senior (and costly) colleagues, whose compensation would be smaller if near retirement age? Or should the last in be the first out? Dare they make lists of colleagues in order of academic merit and take the opportunity to get rid of duds and slackers? Who would decide who was meritorious? Should they bring in outside assessors? Should they take the opportunity to streamline their universities and eject subjects and departments which they felt to be irrelevant, undistinguished or downright pernicious? And if they did not want to reshape their institutions by compulsory means, would the government give enough money to persuade colleagues, preferably the least competent, to go voluntarily?

Universities had to freeze unfilled posts, irrespective of the teaching obligations they still had to meet, and to consider which posts to disestablish. Even though no compulsory redundancies were actually enforced, the *prospect* of selecting those to lose their livelihood created incalculable stress, suspicion, uncertainty and ill will, and generated a vast amount of wasted work and effort.

In facing these decisions academics had not the slightest help from government. Later, a government spokesman glibly suggested that the universities should welcome reduction as an opportunity to reform themselves. But universities could hardly do so when they were required to fit their new financial strait-jackets immediately; every month's salary paid to an academic who was to be eased out of his job meant less money with which to fund the redundancies which would eventually reduce the salary bill and make it possible to keep the university going.

Universities had to make instant decisions about their whole future. Universities are not simple managerial hierarchies, and getting planning decisions agreed with senates, which consist wholly of university employees, is always an enormously difficult task. In the time-scale imposed on them it was simply impossible. They were forced to be opportunistic and accept whatever voluntary departures their staff offered, only rarely turning them down for 'managerial' reasons.

It will take time before the full impact of the decisions on the universities can be assessed. However, immediately after the UGC's letter was received the *Times Higher Education Supplement*, which monitored events with great care, recorded some examples of how the universities counted the cost in human terms of the cuts in their grants. Lancaster University immediately decided to close its first-year course in Russian and Soviet studies in 1981, although six students had been conditionally offered places. Edinburgh University had to ask its bankers for a £3 million overdraft. Imperial College froze all of its new appointments. Liverpool University, which faced a cut of £5 million over two years, also froze appointments and estimated that it needed to reduce its workforce by 300. Salford University estimated that it would need to cut 525 teachers. Bristol would have to lose 145 academic staff in all areas. In some universities teachers began to consider whether they should save jobs by contributing 10 per cent of their salary to the university for a number of years. Warnings of wage freezes were given at Strathclyde.

The cuts were delivered not only in the form of reduced funds but also as reduced student intake figures. The fiction of university autonomy was dismantled. Parkes had written to the Secretary of State that 'although the committee recognises the pressure of the still rising number of applications from well-qualified candidates, it would not wish the recurrent grant of the whole system to be jeopardised by unplanned additional public expenditure at some universities.' This statement shows that the UGC did not ignore the government's wish to keep student grants within certain bounds.

Later, the UGC began to pursue universities which had not restricted their intake of students. These included Dundee, Heriot-Watt, Salford, Bradford, Hull, Keele and Swansea. All but Salford and Bradford were eventually 'fined' for their offence; the UGC deducted the extra fees they earned from grants. Most universities were 'on course' but likely to reach their targets in 1984-85 rather than 1983-84. A few universities were exceeding their targets by at least 5 per cent.

As well as complying with the instruction to cut staff the majority of universities began to shed staff. By the end of 1982 the universities were 45 per cent towards the forecast loss of academic and academic-related staff by early retirement and redundancy. But more than two-thirds who went were professors (20 per cent) or senior lecturers and readers (48 per cent), and there was 'clear evidence that the severance payments for staff under 50 were not proving sufficiently attractive to persuade them to leave voluntarily'. Staff/student ratios had deteriorated sharply because universities shed posts much faster than they reduced student numbers.[6]

The distribution of cuts

The chart on pages 62-5 shows the dramatic nature of the financial cuts. On a 1981-82 price base the recurrent grants made to universities (ie the grants for general expenditure other than on new buildings and major equipment) were to decline from £879.62 million in 1981-82 to £808.07 million in 1983-84. This was a cut of 8.1 per cent in real terms and, added to the cuts already made, represented a total cut of 13 per cent since 1979.

Since the initial announcements, the figures of student losses have become clearer. The universities' peak year for recruitment was 1980-81. Some universities had failed to follow UGC 'advice' to restrain undergraduate first-year admissions in 1979-80, and as a result the total number was up. The numbers of undergraduate and graduate home and EEC full-time and sandwich course students proposed by the UGC for 1984-85 would allow for 23,000 fewer places than in 1980-81 or 18,000 if 1979-80 is taken as the base line.[7]

The *THES* summed up the decision in the words 'UGC Protects the Chosen Few'.[8] No university escaped cuts, but it seemed that 10 of the 45 universities had been protected by the UGC's selective strategy.

The *THES* pointed out that the UGC has always been selective. But now 'in very broad terms, the committee's selectivity strategy adds up to an endorsement of the traditional hierarchy of British universities ... but with a strong and invigorating dash of eclecticism.' The *THES* concluded that with the endorsement of the hierarchy and the suggested subject balance 'the UGC strategy probably corresponds well to the "general will" of the universities faced with

The university cuts announced in July 1981

	Recurrent grant (1981-82 price base)		
	1981-82	1982-83 (tentative)	1983-84 (tentative)
	£m	£m	£m
Aston	12.02	10.77	9.86
Bath	8.88	8.77	8.69
Birmingham	27.83	26.61	25.69
Bradford	11.91	10.60	9.64
Bristol	20.91	20.06	19.43
Brunel	10.16	9.48	8.99
Cambridge	30.03	29.39	28.91
City	9.22	8.66	8.24
Durham	12.13	11.94	11.60
East Anglia	11.71	10.95	10.28
Essex	6.09	5.73	5.47
Exeter	10.77	10.15	9.69
Hull	10.17	9.60	9.19
Keele	7.04	6.23	5.64
Kent	7.42	6.97	6.64
Lancaster	9.36	8.97	8.68
Leeds	30.86	29.63	28.72
Leicester	12.29	12.09	11.95
Liverpool	28.21	27.01	26.13
London Graduate School of Business Studies	1.30	1.41	1.49
London University	181.02	171.76	165.03
Loughborough	12.30	12.11	11.98
Manchester Business School	0.97	0.90	0.84
Manchester	34.53	33.03	31.93
University of Manchester Institute of Science and Technology	13.35	12.04	11.08
Newcastle	22.03	21.35	20.85
Nottingham	19.49	18.84	18.36
Oxford	31.33	30.41	29.74
Reading	13.64	13.07	12.66
Salford	11.85	9.97	8.59
Sheffield	23.25	22.37	21.72
Southampton	17.47	16.97	16.60
Surrey	10.15	9.36	8.78
Sussex	10.27	9.66	9.21
Warwick	12.01	11.56	11.23
York	7.11	7.06	7.02
Total England	699.08	665.48	640.55

Source: Times Higher Education Supplement (3 July 1981)

The university cuts announced in July 1981

	Home and EEC full-time students			
	1983-84 (or 1984-85)			
Arts	*Science*	*Medicine*	*Total*	*Comp 1979-80 Total*
1,080	2,560		3,640	4,670
1,030	2,230		3,260	3,190
3,840	2,790	1,140	7,770	7,750
1,400	2,130		3,530	4,360
2,930	2,620	840	6,390	6,650
850	1,620		2,470	2,460
5,090	4,340	850	10,280	10,490
590	1,430		2,020	2,130
2,840	1,520		4,360	4,530
2,560	1,080		3,640	3,760
1,400	750		2,150	2,240
3,170	1,430		4,600	4,690
3,120	1,080		4,200	5,070
1,570	660		2,230	2,680
2,320	860		3,180	3,430
2,980	940		3,920	4,210
4,070	4,160	1,040	9,270	9,430
2,430	1,260	510	4,200	4,340
2,850	3,060	1,000	6,910	7,060
290			290	170
11,470	12,350	8,400	32,220	33,510
2,100	2,450		4,550	4,670
170			170	120
4,570	3,630	1,510	9,710	9,930
690	2,290		2,980	2,790
2,480	3,060	1,060	6,600	6,880
2,470	3,040	640	6,150	6,380
6,300	3,450	660	10,410	10,700
2,330	2,440		4,770	5,030
740	2,010		2,750	3,940
3,150	2,820	890	6,860	6,860
2,460	2,560	640	5,660	5,690
629	1,850		2,470	2,880
2,440	1,270		3,710	3,890
3,110	1,440		4,550	4,600
1,960	1,130		3,090	3,100
93,470	82,310	19,180	194,960	204,280

| | Recurrent grant (1981-82 price base) | | |
	1981-82 £m	1982-83 (tentative) £m	1983-84 (tentative) £m
Aberystwyth UC	7.34	6.94	6.65
Bangor UC	8.07	7.65	7.34
Cardiff UC	12.48	11.98	11.61
St David's, Lampeter	1.18	1.16	1.14
Swansea UC	9.81	9.30	8.92
Welsh National School of Medicine	4.91	4.80	4.71
University of Wales Institute of Science and Technology	6.30	5.89	5.60
University of Wales, Registry	1.76	1.73	1.70
Total Wales	51.85	49.45	47.67
Aberdeen	17.24	16.06	15.19
Dundee	11.41	10.90	10.53
Edinburgh	31.50	30.75	30.20
Glasgow	30.76	30.20	29.56
Heriot-Watt	7.52	7.27	7.09
St Andrews	8.25	7.82	7.51
Stirling	5.96	5.45	5.08
Strathclyde	16.05	15.27	14.69
Total Scotland	128.69	123.72	119.85
Total Great Britain	879.62	838.65	808.07

Full-time equivalent of part-time degree and diploma, extra-mural and continuing education students

Source: Times Higher Education Supplement (3 July 1981)

the unpleasant, and unnecessary, prospect of contracting resources.'
The one point upon which the UGC was chided by the *THES* was
'the iron link between the level of grant and the number of student
places'. It roundly condemned such a policy: 'We cannot accept that
the protection, let alone the improvement, of staff/student ratios is
more important than the protection, or improvement, of pitifully
low opportunity rates. In the last resort . . . opportunity is more
important than "standards".'

The 10 least affected were Bath, Cambridge, Durham, Edinburgh,
Leicester, Loughborough, Oxford, Newcastle, Southampton and
York. At the other end of the spectrum 'in rough order of misery'
were Salford, Aston, Bradford, Keele and Stirling. These early

Arts	Science	Medicine	Total	Comp 1979-80 Total
	Home and EEC full-time students 1983-84 (or 1984-85)			
1,820	890	—	2,710	2,940
1,250	1,020	—	2,270	2,580
2,560	1,460	360	4,380	4,680
690	—	—	690	710
1,740	1,490	—	3,230	3,340
—	80	610	690	680
800	1,360	—	2,160	2,400
—	—	—	—	—
8,860	6,300	970	16,130	17,330
2,470	1,860	610	4,940	5,140
950	770	760	2,480	2,490
4,310	3,310	1,220	8,840	8,830
3,780	3,640	1,390	8,810	9,100
400	1,720	—	2,120	2,430
1,680	950	250	2,880	3,110
1,460	560	—	2,020	2,470
2,390	3,150	—	5,540	5,790
17,440	15,960	4,230	37,630	39,360
119,770	104,570	24,380	248,720	260,970
			45,480	43,020

reactions of the educational press could not predict the precise impact on universities in the intermediate band – ie those neither struck down nor offered protection.

The results of various judgements converged in the decisions made about individual universities. Twenty-four of the institutions on the UGC grant list did better than the average of 8 per cent (or 15 per cent cumulatively) and 25 did worse. According to the *THES*, a rather heterogeneous collection of universities received protection from the 'punishing rate of decline'. Bath suffered only a 2.1 per cent reduction in its grant compared with Cambridge at 3.7 per cent and Oxford at 5.1 per cent. The mainly civic and redbrick universities had percentage declines in upper single figures, although some got away with less. There was then a broad group of new universities with percentage losses of income edging into double figures. The worst of these were East Anglia with a 12.2 per cent cut (even higher if its recently acquired teacher training commitments are taken into account), and Stirling with a 14.8 per cent reduction. (These figures refer to 1981 and do not include the 1980 cuts.)

But the most severe cuts were made to some of the technological universities, the former colleges of advanced technology which were promoted to help create the white heat of Harold Wilson's technological revolution. Bath and Loughborough were protected, but most of them faced income losses of 15-20 per cent. Aston had to face a loss of income of 18 per cent over three years, in addition to the cuts already made in 1981. Bradford suffered a 19.1 per cent cut and Salford a 27.5 per cent cut. Because of its predominantly arts and social sciences bias, Keele also lost a large proportion of its income. Aston would lose more than 1,000 student places, Bradford 830, Keele 460 – reducing it to just over 2,200 – and Salford, the hardest hit of them all, 1,100. By contrast, York would have stable numbers and Bath a slight increase.

These figures significantly understate the true impact of the cuts because they came on top of earlier cuts. And the reduction in student numbers carried with it, in all cases, a 10 per cent cut in the 'unit of resource', which meant that staff had to go even when student numbers remained stable or slightly decreased. Social science, clinical medicine, pharmacy, biology, architecture, town and country planning and the arts generally shouldered the burden of the cuts. The implementation of the recommendations would lead to a change in the distribution of students among arts, science and medicine from 50:40:9 in 1979-80 to 48:42:10 in 1983-84.

No university was to be closed, though rumours of closures had circulated. Essex, the site of student protests in the early 1970s was alleged to be a prime candidate for closure, but, in fact, suffered 'only' 10.3 per cent.

Apart from the differential treatment of universities, particular theories, embodying the social prescriptions of the Conservative government, were to be found in the allocation letters. Medicine's privileged staffing ratios were ended. The substantial reduction of students in social studies was represented as an attempt to reduce their high staff/student ratios. In February 1983 the UGC warned the universities of the need for special support staff in social studies, but made no financial allocation for such a policy. Universities cut social studies staffing commensurately with student numbers, so no improvement in staffing levels has been recorded. Within natural sciences there was a new emphasis on potentially 'productive' subjects. For example, biology concerned with genetic engineering and derivations from DNA, with important implications for the pharmaceutical industry, were favoured, rather than other equally academically reputable areas of work. Business studies were favoured at the same time as the social sciences in general were reduced.

The Association of University Teachers and the non-teaching unions reacted with anger to the UGC proposals and to the way that they had been excluded from consultations over their members' futures. Rodney Bickerstaff, of the National Union of Public Employees, attacked the 'lickspittle' UGC for acting as the agent of the government. But, in general, public reaction to the cuts was muted.

The Public Accounts Committee under a Labour chairman gave approval of some aspects of the policy. It was pleased that the UGC was being highly selective and trusted that there would be 'adequate consultation with institutions of higher education in the maintained sector to avoid wasteful duplication of provisions'. The PAC also hoped that the UGC would 'bear in mind the desirability of introducing a greater measure of flexibility into future contractual arrangements for academic staff'.[9]

Later, two separate initiatives reinforced the move into recently fashionable subjects. In December 1982 Sir Keith Joseph announced that he was making additional provision, beginning in 1983-84, for training and research in fields relating to information technology.[10] The Science and Engineering Research Council would administer 600 university and 400 polytechnic postgraduate course and research training places. The UGC would receive a grant for an extra 70 university posts, and SERC would be given money for 45 research fellowships. Provision would be made for teaching staff in polytechnics and other maintained colleges. In 1985-86 an extra 2,000 student places, 400 additional staff in universities and polytechnics, and a trebling of research fellowships would be allowed.

A further initiative was directed to maintaining the flow of 'new blood' in terms of university staff. The UGC received a further £4 million recurrent grant in 1983-84 to recruit 230 additional posts, of which 200 would be in science and technology and 30 in the arts and social sciences. A similar level of recruitment would be provided for in the following two years.

These two initiatives would cost an extra £18 million in 1983-84 and £100 million over the period 1983-86. Thus the government moved from expenditure-led policies of cuts towards government-directed changes in the subject balance of higher education. Teachers had been made redundant at great public expense, but new money could be found to appoint new ones in order to follow the fashionable wisdoms of the time. The government did not disclose the labour market requirements on which its information technology initiative was based, or where it thought higher education would find the staff or students for this very large provision.

The allocations made under these dispensations were criticised by the AUT. Some 2,250 applications were received; the UGC announced 312 new posts in April 1983.[11] London was given 42 of the 'new blood' posts and nine of the full-time and one of the part-time information technology posts. It also received four humanities posts – of the kind extinguished elsewhere by the 1981 cuts. Oxford received 16 science and one arts 'new blood' posts and four in information technology. Cambridge gained one arts and 17 science 'new blood' posts, and six in information technology. But Salford University, which suffered badly under the 1981 cuts, was given only two 'new blood' posts and none in information technology. Aston University, which had also been badly hit in 1981, received three 'new blood' posts and two full-time posts and one part-time post in information technology.

The impact on training and research

The 1981 White Paper declared the government's intention 'to give protection to the support of basic science'. The vice-chancellors, however, retorted that it was thus 'shallowly assumed that basic science could be protected when funding for the universities was being run down'. The universities are funded by the UGC to provide teaching and to perform research. They can also get research funds from one of the five research councils – this, together with UGC money, constitutes the 'dual funding' system for research – government departments, industry or other sponsors. But the most expensive assets – a well-founded laboratory, for example – are funded by the UGC for both teaching and research.

Another expensive asset is research time and that, too, is funded by the UGC. Teachers may have student contact for between six and 12 hours a week for as little as 25 to 30 weeks a year. For the rest of their time they are expected to be involved in research and the preparation of their teaching.

The University Grants Committee hoped to impose cuts in such a way that the research capacity of the universities would not be reduced. As we have seen, it kept the cut in the 'unit of resource' down to 10 per cent, in an effort to preserve research capacity and what it deemed to be academic excellence. But the reduction in resources affected universities and departments differently according to the subject being researched. John Ashworth, vice-chancellor of the University of Salford, and a biologist, thought that research costs in his own subject were extremely variable: ' . . . the simple fact that one chooses to work on liver cells and the other on bacterial cells will cause an order of magnitude change in the order of resource.'[12]

Sir Alec Merrison thought that both student numbers and research would be maintained as long as teachers were prepared to reduce the amount of teaching allowed to each student, which was possible in some areas. The universities' research capability was endangered more in the laboratory subjects than in the arts-based subjects.[13]

Lord Flowers, head of Imperial College, believed it to be 'increasingly difficult for a university out of its own block grant plus fee income to support initiatives in teaching or research which have not yet reached the point where you could hope to convince the UGC or a research council [to provide funds]. If your university cannot justify even finding a few hundred thousand pounds a year to back special initiatives in teaching and research, then you are in a position where dual funding has broken down. The university is totally in the hands of external agencies of one sort or the other and has to do as it's told.'[14]

This is the strong case for preserving a generous unit of resource, but the argument was applied inflexibly: accessibility and student numbers were sacrificed to research, yet in many cases research capacity was seriously impaired. No real investigation of whether scholarship and research could have been maintained in non-laboratory subjects, such as humanities and social sciences, was made. It is doubtful whether the unit of resource had much meaning in these areas.

Throughout the period of cuts those in a position to know were deeply disturbed about the prospects for research. A report of a committee under Sir Alec Merrison, published in June 1982, said that research in universities had been under strain for several years and was now seriously threatened by the cuts.[15] A committee of the

Royal Society consulted its representatives on university courts in December 1981 and all of its fellows in June of 1982 to see what damage had been done. The committee considered that the dual system of financing research (whereby the UGC provided the basic resources for research, and the research councils provided further resources for research of established worth) 'was being undermined by the deterioration of the UGC contribution'. It regretted the universities' decision not to follow the UGC in being selective in their cuts. It noted that the 'widespread freezing of vacancies had, in many universities, brought recruitment of able young researchers to a virtual standstill'. The current spate of early retirements was creating an imbalanced age profile. The loss of technical staff and reduction in library resources, on which research depended, were a cause for concern. So was the effect of the cuts in staff and student numbers on both the quality and quantity of postgraduate teaching in science.[16]

Not only had the UGC's contribution to research been reduced. In spite of the 1981 White Paper's declaration of its support for science, the research councils had not been treated generously and the SSRC, as part of persecution by Sir Keith Joseph (see Chapter 10) had had its grants drastically reduced. A good deal of support had begun in the 1970s to flow from government departments acting as customers for research which they might find useful for policy purposes. Their budgets, too, were drastically cut. Private foundations, which had always been able to provide only marginal sums, but which because of their ability to be adventurous and unconventional provided an extremely important additive to the whole research system, also found their funds shrinking during a period of depression.

Leading academics believed the universities' research capability could be put at risk by reductions in their 'core funding', intended finance both teaching and research. The UGC did what it thought best in defence of research, but the policy was applied indiscriminately, through the defence of the unit of resource, to subjects and institutions in which it might have been possible to preserve student numbers with no real damage to research and development. In many institutions and subject areas the way in which the cuts were imposed produced the worst of both worlds: a reduction in the range of courses and the number of students *and* a loss of research capacity.

References

1. Published in First Report from the Education, Science and Arts Committee, session 1981-82, Expenditure Cuts in Higher Education, 2 December 1981, HC 82
2. Letter from Dr Edward Parkes to Christopher Price, MP, 2 November 1981, Procedure Leading to 1981-82 Grant Distribution. And Circular letter 10/81, 1 July 1981. Grant for 1981-82 and Guidance for succeeding years, para 3
3. Education, Arts and Science Committee, minutes, 24 July 1981, HC 499, Q 76
4. Letter from Dr Edward Parkes to Sir Keith Joseph, 16 December 1982, DES press notice 304/82, para 22
5. First Report from the Education, Science and Arts Committee Session 1981-82, op cit
6. Parkes to Joseph, op cit, paras 23-24
7. Parkes to Joseph, op cit, para 15
8. *THES*, 3 July 1981
9. House of Commons, Committee of Public Accounts, tenth report, session 1980-81, 4 June 1981, 233, paras 6-11
10. DES press notice 299/82, 16 December 1982
11. UGC announcement, 12 April 1983, *THES*, 8 April and 15 April 1983
12. Professor John Ashworth, interview, 18 November 1982
13. Sir Alec Merrison, interview, 3 December 1982
14. Lord Flowers, interview, 23 November 1982
15. Advisory Board for Research Councils and UGC Working Party Report, The Support of University Scientific Research, HMSO 1982
16. *Royal Society News*, issue 16, July 1982, p 6

6. The Impact on Institutions

How were the letters announcing reduced grants received? The universities were vulnerable to such radical and instantaneous changes in the level of public funding. They were all suddenly forced to count their money, to accept that they could be instantly in serious deficit, and to look at redundancy and 'voluntary' retirement of academic and non-academic staff as a possible remedy.

The universities were not used to making such decisions. During their period of expansion they tended to follow UGC indications on the broad distribution between subjects, and then allocate staff and other resources according to the number of students that departments attracted. Now they were being called upon to make drastic reductions within two years. It was not open to them to accommodate the change in policy through natural wastage.

Most universities opted for voluntary redundancies, although this inevitably meant uneven departures and reductions in teaching capacity and did not ensure that the least gifted teaching staff would be the first to go. The ablest could find jobs elsewhere and the least able would hang on to their tenures. Moreover, some of the protected subjects, such as engineering, lost a higher proportion of staff through voluntary redundancy.

The cuts in student numbers caused some universities to consider whether to withdraw from the 'clearing' scheme, through which those students who are not given conditional or firm offers immediately are able to be considered once A level results are announced. Aston, for example, feared that it might have to renege on conditional offers already made.

The vice-chancellor at Hull resigned from all of his non-university public offices to concentrate on the university's resistance to the cuts. Other universities, responding to the demands of the UGC that they co-operate with other institutions, began to think about concentrating their own activities on single campuses.

Salford, at an emergency senate meeting 'utterly condemned' the level of cuts proposed for the university. There was an unofficial suggestion that the chancellor, Prince Philip, be approached, and Salford later set up Campus, a system to generate private income, which would make the university more independent of government financing.

Some universities came to special public attention either because their plight was exceptionally dire or because their reactions to the cuts exposed particularly important factors in the whole policy and process. The cases of Salford, Aston, Bristol, Aberdeen and Keele merit particular attention, and here we select two cases for detailed description: Aberdeen and Aston.

Aberdeen shows how a fine university was suddenly thrown into internal disarray by government policy, and how political action mitigated some of the worst features of the cuts. Aston is important because its problems give a good illustration of the issues surrounding tenure.

Aberdeen[1]

Aberdeen is a major Scottish university of impeccable international standing. The medical school, for example, has long had a leading place in the study of pathology and gynaecology. It contributes towards making Aberdeen one of the best-served areas for health services in the country. Its academic departments are thought to display excellence over virtually the whole range from classics to sociology and the physical sciences. It is in the middle of what became a boom town as the oil industry developed in the 1970s. It is a centre of cultural and intellectual life in an area of both natural beauty and potential isolation.

The UGC required financial cuts of over 16 per cent (£3 million) over a period of three years and student numbers were to drop by about 4 per cent. The first guess at the number of required redundancies was 150 academic staff, including clinical teachers in the school of medicine. The whole department of microbiology might, it was thought, have to be closed. By 15 October 1981, the total number of required academic and non-academic redundancies was estimated at between 300 and 350 out of 2,696 staff.

The cuts letter came as a new principal was installed. He set about the task of implementing the reductions in what some teachers regarded as a managerial way. Two other groups played an important role. The Aberdeen AUT opposed the cuts and compulsory redundancies, but tried to make constructive contributions to resolving the problem, even though at times its opposition was strenuous.

But a splinter group, representing those opposed to cuts or accommodation with the authorities of any kind, ran a newsletter called *Alternatives*, which focused the sharper anxieties and resentments aroused by the pressure to apply drastic and immediate measures.

The AUT played a particularly active part. The UGC letter was received at the time when universities put on their best suits and gowns in order to give degrees away, at ceremonies attended by parents and friends of students, and supporters of the university. The Aberdeen AUT sent a letter to parents of graduates pointing out that within four years there would be 20,000 fewer places in British universities, that in 1981 the number of 18-year-olds would be 907,000, and that this figure would rise to a peak of 941,000 in 1983 and remain at 900,000 until 1986. Many qualified applicants for university places could not be admitted, and this trend was likely to be more marked in the north-east of Scotland than elsewhere in the UK. 'Other members of families attending the congregation should have the same opportunities as today's graduates' it said, and the AUT invited parents to complain to MPs.

At the same time, the principal wrote to the UGC to ask if there had not been an error in the calculation of grant. Dr Parkes replied on 28 July that, in determining its level, the committee took into account the higher than average costs in education, mathematical sciences, physical sciences, social studies and arts, and also noted that costs in the medical and dental schools were very high. Thus the UGC took the opportunity not only to impose reductions in capacity but also to reduce the high spenders. The significance of Aberdeen's letter is that many vice-chancellors could simply not believe the cuts that had been allocated to them. Certainly, the UGC allocation letters embodied several things at once. They reduced financial levels far more than the levels of student capacity which they prescribed. They made particularly large cuts in deparments which spent more than average. And they suggested that universities ought both to reduce the numbers of places devoted to social science and to improve social science staffing ratios.

In December 1981 the AUT submitted a paper to the principal which well described the feelings generated by government and UGC decisions. It pointed out that Aberdeen suffered particularly because the cut was 'front-loaded', and that it must make its cuts in 1981-82 even though the grant was not announced until 28 days before the beginning of the financial year. A deficit of £3 million was predicted for 1981. In such a situation factors such as the extremely bad winter had a serious effect on the university's economies, and a geographically remote institution like Aberdeen had additional problems, including high telephone and travel costs. The university reduced the number of its telephone extensions by 50 per cent.

The AUT projected a possible total deficit of £12 million by 1983-84. It prophesied that at 'some time before this point was reached, a receiver would probably be appointed to manage the university's affairs, and to realise the university's assets for the benefit of creditors.' It did not think that the present government could be trusted to change its mind when it saw the prospect of a university bankruptcy. The union therefore accepted that it would be appropriate for the university to try and make cuts this year to restrict its total deficit. It thought, however, that the university's planning committees were producing unduly rigid and over-organised ways of reducing staff and found the set of compulsory redundancies wholly unacceptable.

The union then analysed the UGC's assumption that the university had high unit costs. The rates paid were extremely high in comparison with other universities. The university also had a unique relationship with the Grampian Health Board, and one reason for the size of its medical faculty was that it provided health care as well as medical education. The AUT argued that, when these weightings were removed from the calculation, Aberdeen compared well with other universities which had medical schools. These arguments were never refuted, but the UGC chose to ignore them.

Aberdeen felt aggrieved both at the decisions and about the failure to calculate its revised grants on a logical and equitable basis. But it quickly sought practical ways of reducing its losses. The AUT welcomed the establishment of Aberdeen University Research and Industrial Services Ltd to market the university's consultancy and training services. This private company was also to purchase university assets and then place them on the open market. In this way the university hoped to escape its charter restrictions on the sale of fixed assets. The Treasury, however, vetoed this manoeuvre.

The AUT made a careful inventory of other ways in which the university could generate more income and use its resources better. It thought that cuts of £1.35 million were possible in non-pay expenditure, that income from various sources could be augmented by £265,000 in one year, and that an appeal could raise a further £400,000 a year. These measures would produce a total of about £2 million. It thought that of the £4.3 million reduction in expenditure sought by the planning committee, only £2.3 million needed to come from wages and salaries, rather than the £3.5 million envisaged.

The policy of early voluntary severances enabled the university radically to amend its policy but the AUT document gives a good illustration of the psychological stress engendered by the cuts. The AUT accepted that there must be a reduction in the payroll, but, in the words of its submission:

> It objects intensely to the committee's approach to the reduction. On publication of 'the plan' university employees were deeply shocked and utterly dismayed; latterly the anger has been intense. In producing grids with which to analyse the whole university the committee has successfully alienated the whole academic community; and we are astonished and hurt that 14 academic colleagues have nominated departments for destruction . . . Voluntary schemes must replace the compulsory one, and much work must be done to win the co-operation and trust of staff.

The university hoped that staff reductions would save £0.25 million in the first year. But, according to the AUT, the staffing reductions set out in the report of its planning committee represented 'a major disruption of the academic work of the university'. It continued:

> The activities of many splendid departments and staff of the highest quality will be seriously damaged with the abandonment of successful careers and the likelihood of much human misery. Staff reduction of about 25 per cent overall is likely, and in the case of two departments may be over 50 per cent. This would mean that obligations to students to provide advertised courses would not be met. Because the changes were front-loaded, the period of five years' notice required for a change in course could not be allowed.

Between January and March 1982 the university began to examine particular cases of severance in preparation for a meeting of court in March. The AUT wrote to William Waldegrave to point out among other things that perhaps 170 academic staff would have to leave. The university was experiencing considerable turmoil and collective anxiety. An appeal in February for a change in the grant allocation and student numbers was not accepted by the UGC. The principal wrote to the chairman of the UGC to say that 'news has been received in the university with a mixture of astonishment and resentment.' Because of front-loading 53 per cent of the cuts would fall in 1981-82, and 'savage and potentially damaging cuts' had been necessary in non-pay expenditure. Only negligible savings could be achieved in that academic year through disengagement of academic staff.

The university then had to begin to shed staff. On 23 March the university court decided formally to declare a 'state of redundancy' in respect of academic and academic-related staff. This was a necessary step before the court could enter into consultation with the Aberdeen branch of the AUT about methods of selecting those who might be made redundant.

The university announced that:

> The court's decision has been reached with the very greatest reluctance after months of exploration of ways of bringing expenditure into balance with income following the announcement in July 1981 of a drastic reduction in government grant support. The steps taken by the university to avoid compulsory redundancy have been widely publicised and supported, and included attempts to have the government grant increased in view of the particular severity with which Aberdeen has been treated, reduction of expenditure on non-pay items, offers as generous as permitted by government of compensation for early retirement and voluntary severance, and attempts to increase income from other sources. These efforts will not be relaxed; but the best forecasts available have led the court to conclude that income and academic expenditure cannot be brought into balance without 57½ additional academic and related staff disengagements. The court has therefore decided that it must secure its position by taking preliminary steps to achieve this by compulsion if necessary, but it is the court's intention to achieve this target as far as possible by voluntary means.

But a week later this decision was reversed by senate. The *Scotsman* of 30 March 1982 reported that: 'In what is being hailed as a victory for academic freedom, Aberdeen's senate, the highest academic body in the university, rejected a motion by their principal to "reluctantly accept" the steps that court took last week "to ensure that the essential staff disengagement can take place by compulsion if necessary".' The court is formally the superior body (equivalent to council elsewhere) and its action could have been final. But courts and councils only act on major academic changes with the advice of senate. Before court could meet again on 27 April, the AUT made a series of moves.

It expressed anxiety that Aberdeen looked like becoming the first university to declare compulsory redundancies. It was concerned because of the divergence between the senate and the court over the appropriate policy. It was prepared to co-operate with the university to achieve economies, providing they did not involve compulsory redundancies. But it stressed 'most strongly' the wish to avoid entering into conflict – to avoid costs, damaging litigation and other actions that would be harmful to everybody. The national executive went on in a letter of 14 April to the secretary of the Aberdeen AUT to state the actions it had now agreed. They included: asking external examiners to resign; withholding final examination marks; work stoppages on appropriate days; heads of departments to refuse to co-operate in procedures leading to redundancies; to take appropriate legal action; and to seek reports from professional accountants to use for alternative financial strategies.

These were extraordinary steps for an association representing university teachers to propose, although external examiners (with a few exceptions) did in fact refuse to resign on the grounds that this would be harmful to students.

These remedies, although extreme, revealed the ultimate weakness of university teachers in the face of government. Withdrawal of action as examiners had been threatened earlier, when pay rises had been regarded as too meagre. Even now the AUT could propose nothing more drastic.

The AUT brought in its own accountant to examine the university's books. This proved to be a more useful strategy. The university was happy to co-operate. Ironically, on 30 April 1982 and in the middle of this struggle, the UGC decided to allocate a further £312,000 by way of block grant and compensation for costs on health and safety measures. This would have the effect of reducing the 1984-85 deficit to £1.51 million. Two days later the AUT accountants reported that the funding for 1982-83 was enough to keep the university going in 1982-83. Early retirements had made this possible. A deficit of £600,000 was still predicted for 1983-84. The court therefore decided that, since no emergency would arise in 1982-83, there was a breathing space. This would do nothing to forestall problems in 1983-84, but legal actions and general conflict could be put off in the hope that other measures might emerge in the meantime.

On 5 May the principal was 'delighted' to inform staff that the planning committee had accepted his proposal that court be asked to withdraw its declaration of a formal state of redundancy. An equally delighted AUT informed all local association secretaries. John Acker, the deputy secretary, wrote to them to say that '45 telegrams from local associations were placed before the university court and a very large, silent demonstration, attended by representatives from local associations all over Scotland, was held outside the court meeting. This magnificent display of support greatly contributed to the result of the court meeting yesterday.'

A bitter conflict was averted, but Aberdeen's troubles were by no means over. The university had been reduced to a state of chaos by a series of ill-thought-out decisions administered by government and its agents. The university was left grasping at straws. Other universities had decided that they dare not delay implementing the full-scale reductions if they were to save money in good time and settle down to a new scale of operation. In Aberdeen the conflict had taken a different course, and had produced a temporary respite. But the cuts also made it clear that collegial ways of working were ill-equipped to deal with emergencies. More formal managerial structures would have to be created. Whether the former state of harmony will be restored remains to be seen. The cuts revealed divisions between those totally opposed to attacks on staff tenurial privileges and others who were prepared to see the university slimmed down. It displayed a particularly resourceful amalgam of opposition and compromise on the part of the AUT.

Aston

The problems of shedding staff are well-illustrated in the case of the University of Aston. In September 1981 the university was engaged in talks to find ways of shedding between 120 and 150 academics and 300 non-academics, mainly through compulsory redundancy.[2] It notified the Department of Employment that it planned to make 95 staff redundant. It needed two-thirds of these to have left by July 1982 and the rest by the following year. It had already devised an incentive scheme for early retirement for those aged 50 or over.

The AUT sent a telegram to the vice-chancellor threatening high court action if there were compulsory redundancies:

> The association wishes to record the legal advice it has received that compulsory redundancies cannot take place under the terms of members' contracts and therefore your discussions are of no consequence and serve no purpose. It follows that any attempt to obtain the compulsory redundancy of any member will be opposed by all means available.

The university had been faced with a reduction in its income of 30 per cent by 1983-84 and was thus forty-second out of 45 in terms of the severity of the treatment it received from the UGC. It presented evidence to the select committee[3] that, because of the cuts, engineering would be reduced to subject areas which were currently marketable electronic, electrical and chemical engineering. Production and civil engineering, which would be key areas once the recession was over, would take the brunt of the cuts.

The engineering faculty was distinguished by a close relationship with industry, pursuing sandwich as well as full-time courses and directing a significant part of its research effort to industrial problems. Students had proved to be highly employable. It had been encouraged by the technology sub-committee of the UGC in 1979 to improve its student/staff ratio. Its A level admission standards had risen to compare favourably with the national average for such courses. It ran specialist courses which it could claim were important to areas of industrial and social activity, such as occupational health and safety and chemical engineering, and social science and humanities programmes 'entirely consonant with the ethos and practicalities of Aston as a technological university'.

The departments of applied psychology and modern languages had received accolades from the UGC. The department of educational inquiry, which had an impressive record of funded research, was now 'invited' to close. The university also had departments of ophthalmic optics, pharmacy, construction and environmental health and occupational health and safety, which all offered professional education demanding a knowledge of biology and support from the department of biological sciences.

Aston could make a strong claim that, though some of its A level entrants' qualifications had been relatively weak in the past, they were improving. Moreover, it had sought to recruit students with other than traditional A level qualifications, and could also argue that the 'value added' to many students had proved to be substantial. Its mature students compared favourably with students from sixth forms, and it had long lists of sponsored research on applied problems over the whole range of its subject areas. But those arguments counted for little with the UGC, and the vice-chancellor faced the unenviable task of making massive reductions in staff and students and working on a greatly reduced budget. At the same time, the university attempted to set up a science park which would attract more money and activity.

The university was required to phase out biological sciences, educational inquiry and architecture. Strengths would be maintained in social sciences and humanities, applied psychology and modern languages; the management centre would also be maintained. The vice-chancellor told the select committee that the UGC gave contradictory advice on numbers and departments. It was not possible to follow all of the advice and keep to the numbers that were given. They were incompatible. The university would have an annual deficit of £1.5 million if it did not lose staff.

The UGC had previously visited Aston in 1975. Its Technology Sub-Committee visited in 1979 and the Management Sub-Committee visited in 1981. The Education Sub-Committee had not visited the university since 1970. The vice-chancellor said he felt that the UGC had not had sufficient contact with the university in the recent round of cuts. He felt that technological universities were not adequately represented on the UGC. There was only one such representative on the UGC itself and very few on the sub-committees.

A national scheme enabling the universities to buy out academics who applied for early retirement and who the universities were prepared to let go had been agreed. But this did not relieve universities of the task of ensuring reductions. So, in September 1982, Aston was still faced with the task of reducing its establishment drastically by 1984. The university staff officer sent a letter to every academic at the university. More than 100 received what became known as the 'B' letters, and in four cases they were sent to all members of a department. They were sent during the summer vacation on the decision of the council, but without consultation with unions or staff. A 'B' letter told its recipient that if he wished to apply for voluntary redundancy the university would not stand in his way. 'A' letters were sent to members of staff whom it was deemed could not be spared and to whom voluntary redundancy would be refused. The heads of departments had been asked in confidence to decide who should get which type of letter.

Some heads of department refused to make such a recommendation. In pharmacy and electrical engineering, the heads of departments refused to make a recommendation, so 'B' letters were sent to all members of the department. In another department, where a member of staff had to be selected for the 'B' list, the head of faculty, who had had no intention of going early, proposed himself. In biological sciences the head was asked to name 11 out of 20 for the 'B' list. He refused, so letters went to all. At least two deans of faculty were sent 'B' letters.

By the end of November 1982 the AUT declared its intention of serving a writ seeking a declaration that the 19 to 17 vote by Aston's council to authorise compulsory redundancies was a breach of the university's charter. It advised its members to refuse invitations from Aston to act as external examiners or visiting lecturers if the university pressed on with compulsory redundancies.

The council was to meet on 14 December for the selection of individual staff for redundancy. The union intended to take legal action to force disclosure of financial information, which it thought would show that the financial picture was less bleak than the vice-chancellor had painted. The general secretary of the AUT complained that repeated efforts to discuss the issue with the vice-chancellor had failed. NALGO expressed its support for the AUT action. At the same time, the university was considering wide-ranging changes in academic provision.

If this process had been played out in full, the AUT would have been obliged to have gone to court to seek a declaration that the university's intention was contrary to its charter and statutes. It would also have had to support any individual university teacher who was dismissed. As the *THES* remarked at the time, the main obstacle to breaking tenure would not be legal defences, which sooner or later could be whittled down, but the collegial tradition of higher education with its confusion of employers and employees 'which in terms of industrial relations appear illogical but in terms of intellectual creativity is highly productive'. It thought that few universities would follow Aston's lead in declaring compulsory redundancies. In general, by then, the obstacle of tenure 'had gradually been massaged away by the generous application of early retirement and the restructuring balm. Now tenure is seen as a minor hiccough in a few universities.'

Conflict at Aston was avoided because on 15 December the university council voted that no academic should be declared redundant until after 12 July 1982. Compulsory redundancies for up to 40 lecturers had been proposed, but instead, council called for a full investigation of alternative financial strategies to obviate the need for compulsory redundancies. Aston had already reduced its operating deficit from £1.5 million to £700,000, and it was now argued that the remainder could be offset by reshuffling money currently allocated to development and by savings on maintenance costs.

Aston, like Aberdeen, had to bear the full weight of the government decisions to reduce grants and to let universities find their own way out of the miseries imposed on them by economies. In defending his university before the select committee, the vice-chancellor affirmed support for the whole range of activities in his university. Yet he found himself sending numerous letters to heads of department, persuading or coercing them to fall into line with the government's wishes. The problems he faced were considerable: he was threatened with legal action; many of his senior colleagues would not support the policy which he felt bound to administer to avoid a deficit; and he lacked the political support of the council and the senate to take the steps needed to achieve the projected reductions. This is a striking example of a vice-chancellor being forced out of his old collegial role and into the position of any manager in an enterprise facing recession and sudden contraction.

Academic tenure

One of the major consequences of the cuts was the attack on academic tenure. Universities are idiosyncratic institutions. They exist to produce and to disseminate knowledge and this task has made them unusual employers. It has always been assumed that to engender high-quality knowledge the universities must allow their academic employees a large degree of individual freedom. The freedom has two main characteristics: first, the right, within broad limits, of the individual to determine the nature of his work – his research, the content and style of his teaching, and the way he organises his time – and, second, the right to remain in employment, once appointed on fairly rigorous criteria and subject to good behaviour. It has increasingly been taken for granted that the university teacher will be underpaid compared with professions demanding comparable qualifications, such as the administrative class of the civil service. But, it is agreed, the academic gains compensation for this in the personal rewards that come from having the freedom to work, research and publish throughout his career.

These assumptions have been questioned in recent years on the grounds that, whilst virtually complete freedom and certain tenure have enabled the best to produce fine work, the universities also have to tolerate staff who are prepared to coast along for many of their employed years. The vice-chancellor of Aston University told the select committee in April 1982: 'There are plenty of people who have moved into intellectual retirement at 35.' A previous report of the select committee had questioned the merits of academic tenure. Certainly, in the UK it comes very early in an academic career. A teacher might have taken only three years from graduation to gain a higher qualification, and may then receive tenure two or three years after that.

The enforced reductions made it impossible for the issue of tenure to be avoided. The universities could no longer afford to keep all of their staff. But the great majority of university teachers had been thought safe until 65. Closer examination, however, of individual conditions of service and charters revealed great variations. Perhaps 80 per cent had tenure until normal retirement age. The remaining 20 per cent of contracts were weaker than had been thought. Where the courts were likely to uphold tenure, the costs of getting rid of staff might prove to be high. The main parties involved, including the CVCP and the AUT, sought legal advice, and specialist lawyers quoted compensation figures of between £40,000 and £250,000, with a possible average of £80,000.

The universities were required to reduce in such a way that hasty severances incompatible with rational 'reconstruction' were inevitable. Given, say, five years in which to slim down, there would have been more 'natural wastage', more time in which to negotiate staff losses, and more time to reconstruct academic plans. But the government was convinced that unless it was done quickly universities might find ways of ensuring it would never happen, and that only a fast and radical cut would ensure fast and radical rethinking.

The universities were strapped. They could not simply break tenure. If they were to enforce redundancies there would be painful internal conflicts about who was to go and which subjects were to be lost or reduced. They could lose large sums in the courts. But if they planned, as all did once government-backed compensation schemes were promoted, for reduction through voluntary severance, they risked losing their ablest employees or employees from subject areas which they had been told to preserve. In many universities the age structure was 'wrong'. The older teachers might be in the hard and 'useful' sciences and technologies and the younger ones in those areas most recently expanded, at the UGC's behest, and which had now to be reduced.

The compensation schemes, when finally approved, did not help the universities to cut in all the ways imposed on them, for they offered no continued livelihood to those under 50 but simply lump sums of varying attractiveness. Because the scheme was quite attractive for those over 50, people in their academic prime – the age group which produced much of the best research and writing and many of the best leaders – were being bribed to get out.

There have been no compulsory redundancies so far, but the amount of moral compulsion applied – 'if you go voluntarily we can offer you this, but if you decide to drag yourself and us through the courts we cannot guarantee even this' – cannot be calculated.

The CVCP kept up the pressure on the government to produce a general agreement, based on the existing early retirement scheme, which would negate the claims of those who could seek very large sums from the courts, and at the same time provide equivalent treatment to those whose claim on large compensation was weaker.

In early 1982, more than six months after each university had received its letter outlining the necessary cuts, and nearly a year after they had first been threatened in the Expenditure White Paper, a scheme was authorised reimbursing universities which decided to pay out on early retirement and voluntary severance schemes. Universities were not required to adopt the schemes, but most did so. The University Grants Committee would not reimburse any payments at all if a university offered terms more generous than those of the national scheme. Seventy-five per cent of other costs would, however, be recoverable from the UGC. These would include not only the terms of buying out staff but also provision for 'reconstruction', which included the retention of members of staff for limited periods, usually three years, for a limited proportion of their time, and at about a third of their salaries.

A member of staff over the age of 50 with sufficient service would generally be able to retire with the pension and lump sum for which he would otherwise have been eligible 10 years later. If he had 30 years service he received half salary as a pension and one and a half times his salary as a lump sum. If he had less than 30 years the number of years of entitlement would be enhanced by a further 10 years. Pensions would be index-linked from the age of 55 so that somebody retiring at, say, 50, would mark time on pension for five years but then catch up completely.

Those under 50 could apply for a voluntary severance scheme, which would give them relatively large lump sums according to the number of years of eligible service. In practice, however, only those with secure employment elsewhere would find it possible to live on the proceeds of the under-50 scheme, while those over 50 with sufficient service could retire in comfort.

In facing these problems, the universities received no help from the government. In line with its style of disengagement from the areas of policy where it was prepared to do most damage, the government gave the universities no guidance on how to handle their legal problems. For several anxious months, universities had to begin to consider processes of self-amputation with no certainty that they could find the money to meet the costs of legal action over broken tenures, or of agreements struck with staff persuaded to depart voluntarily. Nor did they receive guidance on how to set about their task as fair employers: whether redundancies should be imposed on the principle of last in, first out; whether those who could benefit from enhanced early retirement (mainly those above the age of 50) should go; whether they should encourage work-sharing schemes, and so on.

None of these questions was raised by ministers or by the UGC. Throughout the first and vital stage of the whole reduction process, the government took the stance that the universities could be treated as totally dependent institutions from which it had every moral right to withdraw resources without prior notice, while at the same time pretending that they were entirely independent institutions able to face up to their own problems.

This was the spirit of Sir Keith Joseph's letter of 5 May 1982[4] to the vice-chancellor of Surrey University, who, with the vice-chancellors of Aston, City, Keele and Bradford Universities, had lobbied Joseph to moderate the cuts. The Secretary of State wrote,

> ... that the one thing the universities cannot do is to assume that the government are bound to come to the rescue; the answer lies in the universities' own hands. The government have already endorsed generous compensation terms for academic staff in recognition of the fact that the majority of them have some sort of tenure. If the staff will not agree to go and cannot, under existing statutes be dismissed, then the only way in which universities can avoid making potentially crippling economies in order to go on paying unnecessary academic salaries is to ask for their statutes to be amended.

Joseph also referred to the 'abuse of academic tenure to protect not freedom but individual jobs irrespective of the consequences to the universities, other members of staff and students'.

Recently, vice-chancellors have been considering schemes for ending or seriously modifying the present system of tenure; the government, too, has taken decisive steps on its own account. The privy council office, on the advice of the DES, had made the approval of an award of a charter to the London University Institute of Education and amendments to the charter of University College, Aberystwyth conditional on changes in their tenure rules. The privy council office wrote to Aberystwyth to say that 'ministers have now concluded that all new and supplemental charters for university institutions which contain provisions on tenure must include in such provisions an explicit mention of redundancy as a reason for dismissal . . . ' Surely, so far-reaching a change should be considered on its merits, and new policies implemented after due negotiation rather than under the duress of instant cuts.

The government had been advised that academic redundancies could cost £200-£300 million. Because of the acceptance of lower compensation under the voluntary scheme, the actual cost was about £100 million. This is still a considerable sum and policy makers should reflect on whether a country is using its resources sensibly in providing £100 million to enable academics, many of them competent and some of them distinguished, to retire in their fifties or earlier, while fewer young people take up places in universities and institutions are reduced in size and scope. Nor can we count the cost of the government's policy, administered with no forethought about a compensation scheme, in terms of wasted ingenuity, conflict and the sense of betrayal within institutions, it produced. It was a rotten procedure, unfeelingly implemented.

References

1. This section is based on publicly available UGC letters and other documents to which AUT headquarters kindly gave us access, and discussions with Dr Raymond McAleese
2. This section is based on publicly available material filed at AUT headquarters
3. House of Commons, Education, Science and Arts Committee, session 1981-82, minutes, 1 April 1982, Q219
4. Sir Keith Joseph to Dr A Kelly, 4 May 1982, DES press notice 98/82

7. Who Did It?
The UGC and the DES

Those responsible for higher education policy had, within a few months, drastically reduced the educational chances of some of our ablest young people. By cutting the range and number of university places they had qualified the Robbins principle that all who were able and willing should find a place in higher education. They had brought about a major reversal of social policy, had dealt massive blows to prestigious institutions, and had deeply demoralised some of the most gifted academics in the country.

Justifying the cuts

The cuts were triggered off unsystematically by radical conservative beliefs in saving money and rolling back the frontiers of the state. They were compounded by politicians' devotion to particular kinds of academic excellence, and by ignorance and confusion about the unintended consequences of social policies. The process of reduction depended more on the mutual reinforcement of many acts of small-mindedness and a lack of liberal intentions towards Britain's young people than on a concerted attack on institutions of learning. It is a story of many Chamberlains and no Hitler. Many of the academics, in the UGC and elsewhere, responsible for implementing the policy, were opposed to it, but they buckled down to implementing it out of a mistaken sense of public duty and a belief that others would do it worse.

Defenders of the government's decision to cut higher education say that it was 'expenditure-led'. This jargon obscures the intention to save money irrespective of the detailed consequences. Those responsible maintain that government 'only' wanted to reduce public expenditure and to protect or even increase expenditure in certain areas, including defence, health, law and order and pensions. It wanted to reduce public expenditure by 5 per cent in 1981, and, since some areas were not to be cut at all, others had to be reduced by as much as 9 per cent. The government felt it had already cut as much as it could in the schools, so savings had to be made in higher education.

Ministers depended on the vague hunch that higher education had expanded so rapidly in the 1960s that, despite the already drastic cuts of the past six years, there must still be fat to be trimmed. It therefore fell out, 'objectively' as it were, that the universities would be required to lose 8.5 per cent of their income, which, with the earlier cuts, and the loss of income from the reduced recruitment of overseas students, took away perhaps 13 per cent of their money within a very short period.

There are contradictions in the accounts given of the way in which decisions were made. The official version implies that Treasury ministers induced a kind of arithmetical determinism, an unconcerned fatalism in their education colleagues. If money must be saved, let the universities help to save it, and worry about the consequences later. Thus Rhodes Boyson, answering a parliamentary question a few weeks after the publication of the 1981 White Paper, said that 'it is not possible to say whether this will mean that any suitably qualified students will be unable to gain access to higher education'.[1]

There was also a feeling within the DES that the universities had not heeded warnings to mend their ways. They had made no response to Shirley Williams' criticisms in 1969, and had continued to believe that government regarded their funding as an open-ended commitment. William Waldegrave summed up the government's dissatisfaction with the universities in a speech in November 1982:

> Not ideology, not monetarism . . . lies behind the squeeze on higher education. The origin lies in the failure of the higher education sector over the last 13 years and more to demonstrate decisively its claim to a protected share of taxpayers' money.
>
> When the squeeze therefore inevitably came, priorities were not set out in time by the academic community itself. Some were imposed from outside as a result, like the decision on overseas student fees. Others had to be constructed within the academic world very quickly, like the decision by the UGC to limit numbers in order to protect research. In one great sector, local authority higher education, the capacity to order priorities itself has had to be constructed only after the squeeze began.

Waldegrave went on to belie the government's claims that cuts had been made solely to save money, and that their academic implications were to be worked out by the academics in the UGC and the universities. He vigorously approved of what had been done: 'We now have heads attached to both the main higher education bodies, and brains inside those heads.' He thought that the storm had been weathered and the worst had not happened, because of the strength and resilience of higher education institutions: 'There will not be the random collapse of institutions across the country confidently predicted to me from across the House of Commons last year.' He also predicted that 'the numbers of those would-be students not finding places in higher education are not going to be at all what was predicted.' But he failed to mention that this was because the polytechnics and other institutions would take far higher student numbers.

Waldegrave expressed concern about the 'new challenges' that faced higher education. Some were external: demographic changes meant that the fall in the overall age group would be just under 30 per cent. There was also a strong utilitarian wind blowing through higher education 'as students accurately assess the needs of a Britain which has a slow long job ahead of it building a better economic performance. This is a chill wind for some of the less well founded arts and liberal studies departments . . . It does pose a great challenge to institutions in meeting legitimate new demands while protecting things which are vital but unfashionable. The third external factor is bound to be continuing resource constraint.' The minister seemed to believe that the strong utilitarian wind and resource constraints came from outer space.

Waldegrave went on to argue for diversification of higher education: 'Senates, councils and governors will have to get used to shifting resources and not over-responding to the lobbies of those who represent the *status quo*.' At the same time he was worried about over-dependence on the centre leading to bureaucratisation, which would rob the institutions of the vigour they needed to respond to challenges. He wanted greater diversification of institutions, and argued that the Robbins policy had led to the wrong pattern: the country could not sustain 44 research universities.

Waldegrave's statement reinforces the impression that government was not only uncaring but also muddled in its thinking. Nothing that the government did encouraged rational new planning. The appeal seemed to be to those institutions under most pressure and with least resources. The older and more esteemed institutions were the least disturbed by the cuts. It was hardly likely that they would respond to the demands for reform.

There is strong evidence of confusion in policy-making. Ministers could not have known how far the universities would be able to meet the cuts out of their existing resources. They simply believed that the universities had been bluffing when they had protested at previous cuts. They did not monitor the effects of the overseas student fees policy before imposing the 1981 cuts. They had no notion of what compensation for redundant academics and related staff would cost. They did not calculate the cumulative effect of their decisions. Even in November 1981, when the chairman of the UGC wrote to Christopher Price, it was not clear whether the policy would produce a reduction in total resources of 11 or 15 per cent between 1980-81 and 1983-84.

Government struck out blindly at institutions which existed to enhance opportunity. Ministers hoped their policies would lead to radical reconstruction. But, because of the existing tenures, the time-scale imposed, and a lack of reflection by ministers, the loss of staff and courses has been patchy. The government took money away but later had to pump some back to meet new objectives, such as inform-ation technology and 'new blood'.

Reducing public expenditure is what Conservative governments are for. But politicians are responsible for the consequences of their policy. The White Paper of 1981, while accepting that the cuts were likely to lead to some reduction in the number of students and increased competition for places, also said that 'the government expect institutions to admit, as they have done this year, as many stu-dents as they can consistent with their academic judgement'. That licence was soon to be revoked by the UGC. But what kind of a government is it that tightens central controls through NAB and acts in a *dirigiste* manner with the universities, but has no view of the pro-portion of each age group which should enter higher education? There is a case for more central planning, but hardly for this kind of perverse serendipity.

At the same time, as the numbers entering the universities fell, there was an increase in the number of students entering advanced public sector courses – up 13 per cent in 1981[2] and 7.5 per cent in 1982-83.[3] The savings in student awards made from cutting univer-sity places was thus lost. The DES had to seek supplementary esti-mates of £36 million and £49 million for 1982-83 and 1983-84 respectively.[4] And, as Albert Sloman had feared, good university courses were closed while less good courses in the same subjects were protected in the public sector institutions.

Is William Waldegrave's claim that there was no ideological intent behind this programme true? Government policy-makers simultan-eously defended what they regarded as excellence – say, classics at Oxford and mathematics at Cambridge – while advancing subjects,

91

such as business studies, that are directly useful to the economy. But the bulk of higher education is neither 'excellent' in the traditional sense, nor directed to the skills thought directly saleable to employers, and the 1979-83 government was not prepared to support education for its own sake. This contrasts with the policy of previous governments, and with Mrs Thatcher's White Paper of 1972, which gave a commitment for the provision of many more student places than the 1979-83 government would have thought useful or desirable.

The University Grants Committee

The government decided its financial allocations and then handed over the making of detailed decisions – which subjects and which universities should be cut – to the University Grants Committee. Once the UGC had decided to sponsor 'excellence' rather than to retain access for the existing proportion of each age group, ministers came round to support the committee's policy.

Sir Keith Joseph's open letter to *The Times* on 12 February 1982 described how the UGC 'took the view that the new level of resources proposed must lead to some reduction in student numbers if quality and, in particular, research capability, were to be protected . . . The government concurred in that view.' He also approved of the UGC's attempt 'to bring about a shift in the balance within the university system as a whole towards more expensive subjects like engineering and technology'.

The UGC was required to make cuts which it did not want to make, and to make them over a time-scale thought unrealistic and unfair. The preferences it exercised, however, once it had decided that it must stay to carry out the government's purposes, reflected its own beliefs about who should get what out of higher education. We can test the UGC's actions by asking how well it resisted government policy, and how far it converted the instruction to cut into measures which were wrong in themselves. We should also ask whether the processes of implementation were compatible with academic ethics.

Weak protest

Did the UGC protest to the government about the tasks that had been placed on it? In July 1981 Dr Parkes told the select committee that the UGC had been allocated funds which were 'certainly not commensurate with their [the universities'] needs, whether they were to remain at their present size or to decline'. The UGC did not, however, at this stage make it clear to the government that the money allocated was not sufficient. It did not do so, Parkes implied, because the UGC had already worked out what would happen to the system in a series of different financial situations. So, it was implied, the government should have been able to infer the UGC's view.

In 1979, however, in the context of a general inquiry about a range of options (see Chapter 4), it had made its views known, both in writing and orally, when the Secretary of State was told that what was to be provided was not sufficient for the needs of the universities. The diseconomies were spelt out to the Secretary of State. 'They were spelt out, in general terms, clearly enough.' When the UGC had advised the Secretary of State on the probable results of the range of options, the 'immediate response . . . was a year of level funding'. The UGC had thought it probable that level funding would be followed by cutbacks, and 'in fact, the worst level which we set was rather better than the scenario that we now have'.

It was reported in the *THES* that Dr Parkes wrote a confidential letter to the UGC sub-committee chairmen in November 1980 which said that there might be less than level funding in the future, and that they must therefore work out a strategy for rationalisation.[5] It might be particularly difficult to provide funds for 'well-founded' research laboratories. The letter went on:

> The committee has concluded, and so advised the Secretary of State, that there are no longer likely to be available the resources fully to maintain the traditional policy of working towards attainment of excellence in as many disciplines as the universities might wish.
>
> It accepts that in the long run smaller institutions may have to concentrate their particular strengths in a limited number of fields. There will have to be more institutional collaboration.

Parkes went on to say that from now on new resources, developments and activities would only be found at the expense of others. In March 1981 the government was told that orderly contraction would be possible if cuts remained at or below 2 per cent but no more. The Secretary of State's response was, apparently, that the money is not there 'in the particular economic situation the country finds itself in'. He was evidently concerned with 'economic' generalisations rather than with consequences. The UGC had warned the government, but whether this constituted sufficient protest is questionable, and the committee's later actions merit even more criticism.

Parkes' view of the 1981 cuts was that: 'The university system can function satisfactorily at any size that any government cares to name. What it cannot do is to change from one size to a smaller size at greater than a certain rate without a good deal of diseconomy occurring. The present rate of change is about twice the minimum rate at which you can do the job in an economic fashion.' This assumption – that it is the rate rather than the fact of reduction that hurts most – is an important part of the case against the UGC. The committee was not, it seems, prepared to do more than mildly demur at the loss of student places or teacher employment.

The central issue is whether the UGC was right to protect 'the unit of resource' – the average amount available to universities for each student – in preference to maintaining the existing number of students. This decision was made by the UGC rather than the government. The evidence is unclear on one important point. We know that ministers, as evidence to the select committee shows, felt uneasy about the scale of higher education, because it entailed both grants to universities and the public sector *and* awards made by local authorities to students entering higher education. Ministers expressed concern that there might be an unlimited run on the local authorities' duty to provide awards freely to all who secured places. The UGC must have shared the government's concern, and this may have conflicted with its alleged freedom to determine how to enforce cuts in grants to universities. In fact, however, even in 1983-84 the government felt unable to restrict student grants because public sector institutions were still being allowed to recruit at will.

William Waldegrave said in a published interview that 'the crucial policy decision ... was not to try and interfere with the UGC. Government policy remains, as always since 1919, to stay at one remove'.[6] He thought that the government would have wanted to adopt the same sort of approach as the UGC's. 'But I am very glad that it was their decision based on the very much greater knowledge and skill that they have.' A kind of reciprocal pride was enjoyed by the UGC. Dr Parkes, in a speech to the parliamentary Scientific Committee, said: 'A number of DES officials said to me after last year's grant letter: "no group of officials could ever have produced a result like that. Even given your information, they would have sought the middle ground, the safe solution. The UGC didn't seek the safe solution; it sought the best solution".'[7] It was this kind of UGC support for government policy that justifies attacks on the UGC such as that made in December 1980 by the AUT president: 'From being the universities' watchdog [a role which Dr Parkes explicitly rejected], Dr Parkes is ready and willing to become the government's hatchet man.'

Access

Was the UGC right to reduce access in favour of sustaining the unit of resource? University resources had already been reduced by 10 per cent as a result of earlier cuts, mainly through the failure to compensate for inflation and because universities sought to maintain student numbers in spite of financial cutbacks.

As far back as 1975-76, the UGC annual survey had referred to 'another year of extreme financial stringency, annual financing and short-term decisions'. A year later, it wrote that the dual support system, by which both the research councils and the UGC contributed to university research funding, was 'under great strain. Because of the cuts in the unit of resource in real terms, research and scholarly work had been a casualty.' In 1980-81, the recurrent grant from which costs such as salaries had to be met, was to continue at the same value in real terms as that for the previous year, while universities took 3 per cent more new home undergraduates than in 1979-80. Admissions varied between subjects. For medicine and allied subjects there was a slight decrease, while the most striking example of university disregard of the committee's advice to hold numbers stable was in mathematics where the intake was 18.5 per cent above that of the previous year. In 1981 the UGC used 1979-80 as its reference point, and far larger numbers of students were admitted in mathematics and engineering but with no increase in funds.

Until 1981, as the real value of grants to each university fell, so the universities either maintained or actually increased their intakes. How much further could this dilution of funding go without damage to academic quality? Could the UGC, for example, maintain student numbers without damaging research capacity? Could the same number of students be accommodated if teachers were prepared to work harder, and would that working harder necessarily have affected performance?

The UGC's resolution of this problem symbolises its approach to the two major policy issues in which it found itself engulfed. The universities must certainly advance academic excellence. At the same time, however, it is they alone who can best advance the social objective of expanding access for the young to the better established and academically stronger forms of higher education.

The UGC decided to narrow access, and to hold the reduction in resources per unit to no more than 10 per cent. However, the unit of resource is a concept far more dependent on its context than on iron logic. We have already quoted the view of John Ashworth, vice-chancellor of the University of Salford, former chief scientific adviser to the government, and the UGC's most severe critic, that it is exceedingly variable in its application to any one area of science, let alone across the whole range of subjects. In the view of another senior vice-chancellor, Sir Alec Merrison, the universities could have sustained both their teaching numbers and their research effort if they had been prepared to reform their teaching by reducing contact hours. The chairman to the UGC himself agreed that the concept was far more applicable to the 'big sciences' than to the sciences requiring smaller accommodation and other laboratory resources, or the social sciences or humanities.

It was the social sciences and humanities which bore the brunt of the cuts, yet their teachers are required to be available for contact with their pupils for no more than 70 to 90 days a year. This does not mean that they necessarily have an easy life, but that choice is far more open than the false rigour of a phrase such as 'unit of resource' implies. Many of them take on a great deal of research, ranging from individual theoretical scholarship to applied research and consultancy related to their academic fields. But a careful analysis of who does what in universities would have yielded enough under-activity for it to have been possible to keep the same number of students, without damage to research, and on a smaller resource base. This applies to institutions of every size and type. Oxford, Cambridge and London, as well as universities outside the 'Golden Triangle', could have yielded more work for the same or less money. But the universities, unlike the public sector, were given no choice at all.

One major science institution, whose student numbers were not to be cut although funds were reduced, decided to continue the same level of research, to take the same number of students, and to allow money for innovation before projects could be picked up by the research councils. It did so by deciding not to maintain its buildings fully while the crisis lasted. Could not all universities make their own decisions on priorities?

The unit of resource is not entirely a meaningless abstraction. It might have had some value if it had been applied with discrimination. But it was applied in the abstract, whereas a course-by-course, department-by-department, university-by-university analysis would have yielded far more flexibility and an ability to maintain student numbers. But the will to attempt such an analysis was not there. There is no reason to believe that the men and women on the UGC did not care for young people. But it is not at all clear that they cared enough, given the challenges which they had to face. It was certainly not their business to help contain the government's commitments to students within prescribed limits.

The UGC's criteria

What criteria were used to determine the institutions and courses to cut? There was a wide range of material available to the UGC: information on the likely numbers of young people coming forward from schools with particular kinds of qualifications; data on the available physical staffing capacities of universities; and information on the number and age structure of teachers in given areas. The UGC knew the type of courses on offer, and the attractiveness of different subjects to particular types of students.

Dr Parkes put these criteria together in discussing how the UGC arrived at balances between arts, science and medicine across the whole system.[8] The UGC looked at the likely availability of students of reasonable quality having different skills, and at the way in which the interests of students and demands of employers were moving. It also looked at areas of science which it hoped would expand, such as aspects of biology with potential economic significance.

At select committee hearings, Parkes admitted to having cut in areas where there was a degree of excellence. But he claimed to have balanced the claims of institutions which took in students with poor A levels but did a first-rate teaching job on them and those which took in high fliers.

The UGC looked first at subject provision and then at the effects on individual institutions. It also fed into its calculations part-time education, which tends to be locally based. It took account of the dichotomy between research and teaching. Parkes claimed that there were absolutely 'no value judgements about institutions'. That is perhaps the most surprising statement of all. Some UGC statements implied a knowledge of what is 'best' and what is 'right', but the criteria recede into the uncertainty of adding up chalk and cheese when inspected in detail, or when one statement is balanced against another.

There is no clear pattern in the treatment meted out. While a mixed group of universities received some degree of protection, those treated worst, with the exception of Keele, were three technological universities: Salford, Aston and Bradford. Several reasons for this have been advanced, and it has been suggested that the work in the reduced departments was academically poor. But the UGC has never clarified this point, and others have attributed the decisions to particular biases among the UGC assessors. John Ashworth refers to the debate that had been going on for several years about the best way of educating engineers. There are those who believe in an education based on design and problem-solving, and those who believe that there should be a compulsory period in industry either before the course or during it.[9] But there are also those who argue the exact opposite – that in the ideal situation 'engineering education in a university is ... not integrated with ... the practice of engineering which will follow it'. This last quotation is from Edward Parkes' inaugural lecture at the University of Leicester in 1962,[10] a time when engineering teaching may have needed academic stiffening. But it implies a resistance to the industry-based, problem-solving type of education which Salford and other technologically oriented universities have tried to promote. It has been suggested that engineering courses placing a higher premium on theory than on work-related practice have been better protected.

There is certainly a problem in university/industry relations in Britain. Stuart Blume, on the basis of his study of chemists, maintains that 'the most academically successful graduates, and those trained in research, do not look to industry with any enthusiasm in deciding upon their careers.'[11] This is because the university sponsors 'a set of values quite divorced from those of industry'. The problem and its solution are complex. But it is not clear that the UGC began to understand, let alone tackle, those problems as it set about its massive reconstruction of the universities.

The criterion of excellence adopted by the UGC and applied in its narrowest form conflicts with the concept of 'value-addedness'. A university may start with students with relatively poor A levels and advance them considerably. Universities such as Salford have, in the past, taken poorly qualified students and helped them become graduates who do well on several indices of performance, including employability. The A level criterion is viewed quite differently in different parts of the system. At Oxford, for example, the great majority of the entrants obtain excellent A level scores, but the colleges leave open a majority of places for those who succeed in college entrance procedures. They are then given an offer of entrance, conditional on only two E grades at A level.

In a letter to *The Times*, a member of the University of Aston's mathematics department showed that 40 per cent of those who had received first class honours degrees and 69 per cent of those who had received second class honours degrees in mathematics in the past 10 years would have been excluded from Aston on the criteria which the university was now compelled to adopt. The experience of the department has been that 'it is quite possible for a student to enter with two grade As in mathematics and then fail the course, while another student with grades D and D obtains a first class honours degree.' Others take a less radical view, but all accept that A levels are an uncertain predictor. One leading science academic said: 'People who have four As tend to get firsts and people who have four Ds tend to get thirds or fail. But there is a great deal of difference in the middle, and anyone who thinks he can predict the difference between a 2(I) and a 2(II) student on entry is just talking rubbish.'

A further criticism of the UGC concerns its failure properly to understand the nature of the process of reducing the system. Dr John Ashworth argues that Parkes and his colleagues felt that contraction would be the same as expansion and that all they have had to do was to change the signs in the planning equation. The social processes are 'profoundly and fundamentally different' from mathematical formulae. During a period of expansion, Ashworth suggests, the UGC was absolutely right to plan policy on a subject basis, but this approach was inappropriate in a period of contraction.

Some critics suggest that this is one of the reasons why the UGC should have resigned. It was not equipped to scrap courses or dismantle departments in universities, nor was it able to cope with the impact of its decisions on individual institutions. Established in a period of expansion as an honest broker between government and the universities, it could not suddenly become an all-powerful arbitrator.

The consultation process
Evidence to support the UGC's claims that it undertook thorough consultation is patchy, and it is doubtful whether the process was as comprehensive or the information collected as complete as the UGC has suggested.

The UGC was required to act with great speed. The Expenditure White Paper appeared in March 1981. It demanded decisions that would require universities to shed staff from the autumn of 1982, if they were to meet the timetable and scale of reductions imposed by the government. The UGC had just over three months to announce the relevant financial allocations if the universities were to have a year – no more – in which to determine their future structure, admit a reduced number of students (whose applications would need to be considered in the autumn of 1981) and plan all necessary economies.

In spite of this time-scale, both the UGC and those who appoint it in the DES felt it consulted thoroughly and with appropriate results. But no systematic internal investigation was attempted. The UGC depended entirely on submissions by vice-chancellors and senior university staff. Moreover, the exercise was conducted within a hypothetical planning game based on assumptions far different in scale from the cuts actually imposed.

How could a vice-chancellor make an assessment of his staff in every subject? What kind of internal analysis backed up this process? The personal experience of one of the authors suggests there was very little. He has been head of a department in a new university since 1970, and was a member of senate, yet hardly noticed these negotiations, in retrospect so important. Other members of university teaching staff will confirm that the vast majority of them did not either.

There are no systems of university evaluation or programme review in the UK similar to those which operate, sometimes as a mixed blessing, in the USA. The CNAA, which has an organisation designed to assess courses in non-university institutions, finds it difficult to evaluate whole institutions, and is chary even of evaluating courses other than to say that they pass the criteria for the award of degrees. It would not dare to rank them, even though it has access to far more data and much greater experience of evaluation than the UGC.

The UGC claim to have made a thorough assessment of the universities during this period of negotiation is therefore untenable. At most, it could have formed an assessment of the thinking of the vice-chancellors and of *their* quality.

The second claim made by the UGC is that the members of the UGC and of its specialist sub-committees 'know' the state of their subjects. It has also been said by a member of the UGC that this knowledge is more precise in science and technology than in the arts and social studies. It is certainly true that scientists live by the learned journals in which, year by year, a competent academic will note the constant flow and majestic progress of his subject area as knowledge is added little by little, as old knowledge is tested, reformulated and improved. A typical judgement made by a member of the UGC was that one department being cut taught science that would have done it justice in 1910, but not now. Such judgements can be formed, but only with hard work. It is questionable whether any group of people, working with the data and time available to the UGC and its sub-committees could have made such evaluations, for the whole range and number of departments. Academics on the sub-committees were required to cover a wide range of subjects. It is one thing to know that so and so has published six articles in molecular biology. It is quite another thing to make an evaluation, on a Sunday evening at home and on the backs of envelopes, in preparation for a meeting which has to be got through by lunch-time on a Monday, about a whole department. It is simply not feasible that one academic would, without devoting months or even years to the task, be able to reach judicious evaluations of what is best in a subject discipline covering 44 departments and perhaps 400 academics.

Again, it is fair to quote one's own experience. Two of the disciplinary areas with which one of the authors is concerned are social policy and administration and political science. These areas are covered, on the UGC sub-committee, by two distinguished and entirely responsible academics. But to evaluate departments, the political scientist for example, would have to know the state of work in political philosophy, political behaviour and psephology, the politics of different national systems, international relations, British political institutions, modern developments in policy studies and policy analysis, developments in the study of the EEC and other regional studies, and public administration. A professor of political science would certainly expect to pick up some knowledge of all of these subjects, but he would never claim to be able to rank, in order of merit, the departments covering this range of subjects.

Moreover, the authors have been told by some of those involved in the process that members of the sub-committees did not feel fully involved in building up evaluations in the way that has been suggested by the chairman of the UGC. Their chairmen were all members of the main committee, but that would give them access to summative judgements, again imperfectly formed, about whole institutions rather than judgements on subject departments.

The UGC's knowledge of a whole university has also been questioned. Could members know enough about the institutions, given the somewhat haphazard nature of their visits? Dr Parkes told the select committee firmly that visits are not intended for evaluation. A university or department not visited for 10 years can be evaluated by other means. Other senior academics we interviewed also believe that visits are inefficient ways of discovering quality, and that their main purpose is to make the UGC and its sub-committees known to the universities. Also, in the one-day discussion which a visit usually entails, members of the UGC can get a feel for the problems that are affecting a range of universities.

While accepting these arguments, it is unlikely that visits do not contribute towards evaluation. That may not be their declared aim, but it must be one of their effects. Is it possible *not* to form a judgement if the committee asks for a batch of papers stating the view of an institution and its department of their present state and future plans? Why are lists of members of departments and their records and lists of publications asked for in advance of visits? The statements on this aspect of the UGC's work are again confused and misleading.

Whether or not the UGC felt that the visits were part of the evaluation process, it must have been aware that this was certainly the view of the universities. The subject sub-committees, according to the UGC's own submissions, were given, to quote the *THES* (7 August 1981), 'a new, far more positive role in advising how the cuts should be implemented'. But they had 'woefully out-of-date first-hand information'. The UGC stressed that they had examined subject provision over the whole system rather than looking at institutions, but that subject provision was never scrutinised through site visits. The UGC letters to universities had to be written in a hurry, but they showed quite considerable ignorance of the way in which some universities operated. A UGC letter to Keele claimed to endorse university proposals for a shift of emphasis from social studies to the arts. The university retorted: ' . . . that is absolutely wrong. We have never suggested any sort of shift.'

The UGC felt it must move quickly and therefore on the basis of imperfect knowledge. In that case, however, the implicit claims that it went for what Dr Parkes described as 'the best' – and his statements before the select committee imply that by and large it knew what was good and what was less good – should not have been made. There were value preferences made which depended on academic preferences rather than on a precise analysis of institutions, departments and the policy choices open to the UGC.

Advice from outside bodies

Further questions arise on the UGC's claim about the advice it took from external bodies. It claimed to have received

much useful information and advice from research councils and
other funding bodies, from the Royal Society and the British
Academy, from the Committee of Vice-Chancellors and Principals,
the AUT and the NUS, from employers and graduates, and from
other organisations and individuals. We are very grateful to all of
those who have offered advice but for our conclusions the committee
alone is responsible.

But it is quite difficult to piece together what did happen, and
again the UGC has implied more consultation than in fact took
place. It is known that the chairmen of the five research councils and
the chairman of the UGC had one or more meetings, at which they
were asked which university departments should be protected from
the cuts. It is also on record that the Science and Engineering Council
presented the UGC with a list highlighting the best and worst centres
for attracting science grants.[12] It gave the number and amounts of
grants made to universities and their ability to attract funds. The
THES reported concern among SERC officials that this information
might be used to measure the quality of departments or even be used
as a basis for closing some down. The SERC also warned universities
in August 1981 that they would receive grants only if they obeyed the
UGC's instruction to cut. Certainly Parkes informed the universities
in May 1981 that 'the committee decided that particular attention
must be paid to retaining capacity for research, and there have been
consultations with the research councils to this end'.

Parkes' letter to universities had said that '... for our conclusions, the committee alone is responsible'. Yet it seemed to imply
that many expert groups were consulted and that their thinking contributed towards the committee's decisions. We cannot tell whether
there was a systematic process of consultation with 'experts', nor can
we be certain of the extent to which elements of that process
reinforced the policies which the UGC reached.

An example of the difficulty in assessing what advice went into the
UGC's calculation is that of its relationship with the Royal Society. It
seems unlikely that the UGC formally sought advice from the Royal
Society, but it certainly received advice from it all the same. That
advice pointed to the need to sustain the kind of university system for
which Britain's elite science body was bound to press. Significantly,
39 per cent of its fellows were at Oxford and Cambridge, and their
approach was naturally a highly conservative one.

In November 1979 in his presidential address, Lord Todd, reverting
to a theme that he had long advanced, referred to matters such as

problems arising from the age structure of university staff, the balance between research and teaching and the need for excellence, and advocated diversity in British universities.[13] In July 1980 the Council of the Royal Society submitted evidence to the Advisory Board for Research Councils on the support for university scientific research, and its proposals implied the need for 'greater discrimination and selectivity within the university system and an increased emphasis on excellence'. Between March and May 1981 there were individual contacts between Dr Parkes and Sir Andrew Huxley, president of the Royal Society, and the society's previously expressed views were reiterated. And the same process was confirmed in a letter from Sir Andrew Huxley to *The Times*, which said that the Royal Society had given advice and had said that the UGC should support excellence.

Later, the Royal Society formed an *ad hoc* committee to monitor the effect of the cuts once they were announced. It consulted Royal Society fellows throughout the country about the effects that the cuts were having in their subjects areas, not only in their own institutions but also elsewhere, and concluded that the cuts were, in general, having a disastrous effect.[14]

The bizarre episode of consultation with the engineering institutions exemplifies the insecure nature of making such life-and-death judgements. A report in the *THES* on 20 August 1982 stated that Dr Kenneth Miller, director-general of the Engineering Council and a member of the UGC, claimed to have consulted people in the engineering institutions about the proposed treatment of the universities. The report caused a vice-chancellor to ask the president of one of the engineering institutions whether there had been in fact any secret dialogue between the engineering institutions and the UGC. If so, what did the institution say about his own university? He was told that there was no formal link between the UGC and the institution, and that it had not been consulted by the UGC prior to the publication of its recommendations. Nor had it at any time divulged details of accreditations of individual university departments.

Co-operation of a different type was reported later when in August 1981, SERC warned vice-chancellors that departments failing to provide acceptable laboratory facilities would lose their grants. This message was interpreted by the *THES* as supporting the UGC's aim to impose selectivity in giving grants. SERC also withdrew grants and studentships from three departments at Aston, Bradford and Sussex, the closure of which had been proposed by the UGC.[15]

All these illustrations show that much of the consultation was haphazard and arbitrary. Claims to have consulted were advanced and a false authority attributed to the judgements reached. But the university departments being cut could legitimately raise several questions about the process.

Consultations were secret and accounts of them are contradictory. The departments that suffered cuts are entitled to know who did or said what. Both natural justice and academic ethics demand that those being assessed know who is assessing the quality of their work and the basis on which that judgement is being made. Secret consultations are unacceptable, particularly among an academic elite which is supposed to advance knowledge and truth. The UGC's description of its earlier consultations with universities and the learned bodies may have implied an exaggeration of the quality and amount of advice received. Even if these bodies were consulted, and so became party to the decisions reached, it was fundamentally a bad process.

While the research councils, to take the most important example of those consulted, make many important judgements, based on expert knowledge, of people in their field, they do so in specific contexts. They judge them for the award of research grants and for postgraduate studentships. But it is commonly assumed that it is the UGC which knows about whole departments, for it is responsible for 'core' funding for teaching and research and brings them to the state of competence to receive research council funding. Research councils will be more inclined to favour the best-established departments rather than those on the way up. Moreover, research councils vary in the attention which they give to new kinds of knowledge as opposed to that developed traditionally within the disciplines. For example, one of the strongest research councils, the Medical Research Council, is competent in promoting biomedical research but has been backward in using its resources to solve the problems of health services research, and social or community medicine. (It was for this reason that the government reduced its funds, under the terms of the Rothschild report, between 1972 and 1979.) Nor do research councils know about the general teaching competence of departments. And it must again be emphasised that undergraduate teaching is one of the main roles of universities and colleges.

Academics on any of the committees of a research council can form judgements on which department is best at a particular kind of research. They have to make judgements about which departments

105

should receive research students because they hand out the student-ship quotas. Even so, they should be reluctant to judge the quality of departments' teaching, research, scholarship, consultancy and gen-eral competence and usefulness or to put them in rank order. How, then, could a chairman, no matter how distinguished, and one or two officials do so? And how does this process of making judge-ments square up with the confidence placed on distinguished col-leagues by the rest of the academic system?

Moreover, whilst the research councils, professional institutions and learned societies can speak for science and technology and for elite academic humanities studies, none of them spoke for other stakeholders in higher education. The Royal Society did, in fact, attack the reduction in the access for young people implied in the government's decisions as translated by the UGC. But none of these bodies is primarily concerned with the access for young people. This is not their primary concern. They would be bound to advance the claims of particular forms of scientific research and excellence in particular fields or argue for the training of people who might appeal to restricted groups of employers.

The less elite professional bodies were not consulted. In recent years there have been strenuous efforts to advance the quality of teaching and research in social work. One of the effects of the cuts in higher education was severely to damage advanced social work courses. But the Central Council for Education and Training in Social Work, which is responsible for the qualification of social workers, was not consulted. Nor did the DHSS, the government department concerned with the training of social workers, partici-pate in the process; perhaps they were not invited to comment.

The degree of consultation was over-stated to the point where a kind of moral support was inferred which the UGC was not entitled to claim. The criteria being applied were not those of young citizens' rights to access to higher education but the narrow needs of a govern-ment concerned with productivity and the equally narrow criteria of those concerned with scientific excellence. And, wittingly or other-wise, the academic leadership colluded in this process because in different ways academics shared the government's preferences, even if they disliked the methods.

It has been argued that the members of the UGC do not represent the whole range of subjects and institutional types, and that those who were hit hardest – the technological universities – were under-represented on the committee. That is a less serious charge than many of the others. The chairman of the UGC had been a vice-chancellor of a technological university. The most prestigious of our universities are also our largest. It would certainly be unfair to assume that any member of the UGC would go out of his way to support the claims of his own institution. There are well-known and rigorously used procedures for excluding a member of any sub-committee when his own institution is being discussed.

The more relevant criticism is that many of the members were simply inexperienced for the job they now faced. While the UGC was expanding universities, a politically inexperienced academic of high distinction could play a useful part in satisfying himself that academic distinction was not being ignored in the calculations. But the job of coping with contraction demanded very different qualities. The process was inextricably tied up with social and political judgements which could not be brushed aside. Dealing with the impact of cuts on institutions demanded skills and sympathies learned in the cut and thrust of educational politics. In this respect, members of the UGC were not selected for the job they had to do.

Resign or collaborate?

What should the UGC have done in the face of the burden placed on it by ministers? Edward Parkes seriously considered resignation, but he and his colleagues, when questioned in the select committee, were clear that if they did not make the reductions, the DES would do so itself on criteria that might be even more unacceptable to academics. One vice-chancellor described this as a 'tired commentary' on the crisis facing the universities. There are counter-arguments. A refusal to collaborate would have made life far more difficult for the government. The UGC and vice-chancellors could have declined to collaborate on the grounds that a moral contract had been established between higher education and the government, and that government should at least give the universities a decent period of notice before winding down obligations to young people wishing to enter university and to tenured colleagues. Or it could have refused to act until the government had showed its hand on compensation for tenure and revealed its plans for the public sector. The DES could not be resisted in the end, but could it not have been compelled to face an explicit revolt and the resulting political row?

UGC members disliked government policy. But they seemed prepared to take on a socially indefensible policy, and make it credible, by agreeing to do what, as we have shown, they were not really competent to do. The result was that injustice was manifest, not so much because of the injustice of individual decisions but because the process itself was not legitimate. Parkes agreed that decisions were made in a hurry and that mistakes might have been made. But there is an indefinable aura of smugness and complacent certainty of judgement running through his evidence and through the *ex post facto* justification in his speech to the parliamentary Scientific Committee. It should have been no comfort to the chairman of the UGC that what he did found favour with destructive ministers or their advisers. He exuded the feeling that reduction was the right solution but was being imposed by government in the wrong way.

In addressing the CVCP in October 1980 Parkes said the universities had exceeded their recruitment target by 3 per cent. 'If you are scraping the barrel in the belief that money follows numbers then you have been unwise.' Scraping the barrel? 1980 was a bumper year for school-leavers. The priorities implicit in this phrase are those of an economising bureaucrat rather than an academic with concern for the range of opportunities of the young. The committee's decisions, though perhaps well-intentioned, did favour the well-established institutions and showed little sympathy for the less well-established forms of academic life struggling to get off the ground.

The UGC's statements imply regret that over a decade perhaps several tens of thousands of qualified young people will not obtain university places because of this round of reductions. Those who fail to get places will compete with others in the employment market, leaving an even weaker group to be added to the dole queue. In spite of all of this the UGC preserved a hypothetical notion of the unit of resource at the expense of young people's opportunities.

Those who provide higher education have to guard the sacred flames of academic excellence and elegant science. They also guard the cash registers of opportunity; admission to a university remains one of the few prizes that competence and motivation can win for 18-year-olds in Britain today. The UGC of its own will, not the government's, made the currency harder. In largely exonerating the UGC from what it did to implement government-inspired cuts which are 'as senseless as they are vicious', the *THES* could not accept the 'iron link between the level of grant and the number of student places'. It went on: 'We cannot accept that the protection...of staff/student ratios is more important than the protection, or improvement, of pitifully low opportunity rates.' That was well said. A particular blend of elitism and an unacceptable process of decision-making produced a bad social policy.

References

1. Rhodes Boyson, answer to parliamentary question, 6 July 1981, *Hansard* HMSO
2. *DES Statistical Bulletin 9/82*, Higher Education in Great Britain: Early Figures for 1981-82, table 2
3. NAB 21/83, paper by DES, Implications of the Government's Expenditure Plans for Local Authority Advanced Further Education, table 2
4. DES Estimates 1983-84, class X vote 2, para 6, p 10
5. *THES*, 28 November 1981
6. *Edinburgh Bulletin*, interview with Ray Footman
7. Reported *THES*, 17 December 1982
8. Select committee minutes, 23 July 1981
9. J M Ashworth, 'Reshaping higher education in Britain', *Royal Society of Arts Journal*, October 1982, No 5315, Vol CXXX
10. Dr E W Parkes, *The Education of an Engineer*, Leicester University Press 1962 (quoted by Ashworth, op cit)
11. Reported in *THES* 4 September 1981
12. *THES*, 15 May 1981
13. *Royal Society News*, No 1, January 1980
14. Ibid, No 16, July 1982
15. *THES* 14 August 1981

8. The Best Lack All Conviction: Higher Education Caves In

The 1979-83 government attacked higher education without real thought about the consequences, and the UGC implemented government policies too loyally and on particularly narrow and socially unresponsive criteria. But how did they get away with it? Did education defend itself properly? And, if not, was that because some academics were predisposed to the restrictive government policies? Did higher education have any friends? Did it receive, and deserve, support from outside?

Differences of opinion

The academic elite was, with a few notable exceptions, hostile to the cuts and even more to the speed and random savageness with which they were imposed by the government. But in many ways it showed itself ambivalent on the main issue raised by the government's action: whether to defend the extension of opportunities for young people that had taken place since the 1950s. Some academics were not disposed to do so, for they had attacked the expansion and the size of the system long before the government moved against it. And a small minority were prepared to turn Queen's Evidence against what they regarded as morally and intellectually suspect parts of their own peer system. When faced with the implementation of cuts, vice-chancellors found themselves dragged into making reduction feasible rather than demonstrating loyalty to the academic creed of support for colleagues' rights and the social objectives of wider access.

Ambivalence about expansion had been expressed openly and frankly by a few leading academics. The rector of Imperial College, Lord Flowers, has declared publicly that there are too many universities, and that expansion took place much too quickly.[1] But he has also protested that the reductions took place too quickly.

In 1975 the vice-chancellor of Birmingham University, Dr Robert (now Lord) Hunter called for special treatment for Birmingham, Leeds, Liverpool and Manchester to maintain their leading position in research and advanced degree courses. He warned that the country's economic recovery was being jeopardised by the educational policy of spreading grants and resources across the board. 'We have earned, and in the national interest deserve, special treatment in the way of provision of staff and resources. This is elitism against the current vote-catching egalitarianism.' He and Jo Grimond, on the same occasion, said that some universities and polytechnics might have to be closed so that a few quality institutions might be maintained. Norman St John Stevas, then shadow spokesman on education, described this as a counsel of despair, and Arthur Armitage, chairman of the CVCP and vice-chancellor of Manchester University, declared it to be absolutely contrary to the needs of higher education to close any university or polytechnic. This view was supported by the vice-chancellor of Liverpool University.[2]

These differences of opinion had been present from the beginning of expansion. While the UGC had earlier been worried about the effect of expansion on the universities, few resisted expansion after Robbins had established it as the political orthodoxy. Kingsley Amis might have proclaimed that 'more will mean worse', but most thought that more would also mean more – more higher education for a larger number of qualified students. In 1964 A H Halsey conducted a survey of university teachers. Two-thirds thought that more would mean worse, but that did not mean that all were opposed to expansion. He went back to the same sample in 1974, and only 46 per cent still held that opinion.[3]

Most of those who had looked closely at the issues believed that expansion had been the right policy. It had brought in its wake not only a quadrupling of the access to higher education (if we include polytechnics and colleges as well as universities), but also some good new universities which took their place as international centres of teaching and research. And even with this rapid expansion, Britain still lagged behind most other developed countries in what it provided.

The conflicting views of the aims of higher education are derived from the fact that universities, and to a lesser extent, polytechnics and colleges, are concerned with two linked but potentially diverging functions. They must create and test new knowledge, and they must educate the next generation of people who will take up key positions in society and the academic system itself. The Robbins report assumed that many more students could be recruited to higher education without damage to research and scholarship, but was mainly concerned to ensure that able young people be given access to higher education.

While the majority of university teachers feel that more did not mean worse, the consent of elite academics, including some who became vice-chancellors, was only given on the condition that they would not be affected by the increase in numbers. Professors in the hard sciences and humanities, or in the prestigious universities (and not just Oxford and Cambridge), could protect themselves from contact with students falling within, say, the lower two-thirds of those who secured two A level passes. They would teach those with As and Bs and need pay no concern to 'adding value' to those who gained lower grades.

Many leading scholars paid little attention to the teaching needs of such young people. They might protest that they cannot both aim for Nobel prizes and worry about improving the scientific grasp of those who present themselves with two Cs and a D. But this *is* a responsibility placed on teachers and heads of academic institutions. They should either hand over the task to others, or do it properly themselves. Perhaps the ablest academics are not the best people to mould higher education policy, and lead higher education institutions. These tasks require a belief in broad educational principles, and an understanding of the needs of young people whose full promise may be late in developing.

Some academics, and not only those from the five or six most distinguished institutions, took the view that the universities should not be taking those with Cs and Ds at all. This view could be found at all levels of the academic enterprise. The engineering professors, for example, called for a reduction in student numbers at their 1981 annual assembly. Some junior staff, as well as the senior elite, would be concerned to preserve the unit of resource and to uphold or even improve A level entry standards. They argued that less well-qualified students belong to the polytechnics, but they have never explained why they are unable to work with students who achieve Cs, Ds, or Es. These are not fail marks and still represent achievement of levels to be expected of young people within, perhaps, the top 10 per cent of the age group. This attitude also ignores the fact that young people change, and that many are at schools that can no longer provide the full resources for good sixth forms. The concept of 'value addedness' is not recognised by those who have presided over the most favoured parts of the system.

A few academics made speeches supporting, and perhaps encouraging, government policy. In March 1981, in a debate in the House of Lords, Lord Swann, formerly vice-chancellor of Edinburgh

University, suggested that universities were unpopular in the public mind, perhaps because they had failed to fulfil the unrealistic goals set for them in the 1960s.[4]

Others have made statements about what they consider to be the lowering of standards. Lord Vaizey, an academic ennobled on the recommendation of Harold Wilson, expressed doubts about expansion in the late 1960s and said in *The Times* that 'the pupils I received from them [the inner London comprehensive schools] at the university were often barely literate'. A survey of the previous four years of graduates in the school of social sciences of which Lord Vaizey was then head showed that his inner London comprehensive school students had, in fact, performed better than the mean. In March 1981 Lord Vaizey told the House of Lords that the universities had brought many of their present problems upon themselves. Student/teacher ratios were unreasonably low, and there was an urgent need to coordinate courses and look carefully at the allocation of resources.

The clearest examples of senior academic backing of government attitudes are the statements made by Max, now Lord, Beloff. Lord Beloff was formerly professor of political institutions at Oxford. He founded the University College of Buckingham, is a Fellow of All Souls, Oxford, and was knighted and then ennobled by Margaret Thatcher within two years of her taking office. He has a long record of resisting both government intervention in universities and the widening of access. For example, he deplores the fact that undergraduate entrants at Oxford no longer have to pass an examination in both a second and a classical language. He represents these as 'hard' subjects, although the standards of A level examinations in all subjects are markedly more difficult and taxing than those taken for the higher school certificate before it was abolished in 1950.

The standards now demanded of candidates at Oxford and Cambridge also go far beyond those required in the 1950s when the colleges had their full share of dolts from the public schools, up for the sporting life and looking forward to a lower second or a third in history or law on a few hours work a week. This point was unwittingly confirmed by Professor Geoffrey Elton in a letter to *The Times* (14 February 1983), in which he blamed the pressure on Oxbridge places on the egalitarians. In his day, the best, he claimed, often went elsewhere and liked it. Elite academics certainly inhabit a world of fantasy and nostalgia, for many of the best or the good were excluded from Oxbridge places through traditional school-college connections. They hardly stayed away out of preference and very many young people have always been aware of the educational, social and job advantages that Oxbridge confer on its graduates. Those advantages will increase as the less favoured institutions become increasingly demoralised and poorly funded following the cuts.

With these predispositions against the Robbins principle Lord Beloff has moved on to tackle broader issues. In a debate in the House of Lords in February 1982 he again attacked the total dependence of universities on government finance. He thought that the system of funding had 'put at the head of nearly all of our universities . . . people who were chosen as vice-chancellors not for originality or for strength of character, but because of their ability to deal on friendly terms with the providers of state money'.[5] He did not think that the cuts had gone beyond 'cutting off the fat'. One example Beloff cited is that £20 million a year went to subsidising student unions. He thought that many of the troubles in universities were derived from the fact that 'we clearly allowed to slip through this net a number of students who [are] wholly unsuited to a university environment'. The Robbins principle was more an ideal than a principle of action. And he thought that there was 'fairly general agreement that it would be a pity if this round of cuts left us with fewer technologists and more sociologists'.

Such statements as these do not justify belief in a reactionary conspiracy in favour of restricted entry. Rather they display a desire on the part of some academics to fall in behind hard-line, if confused, restrictive policies. The House of Lords has several active academic members, who mainly owe their present status to the benefits conferred on them by academic work. But from March 1981 the House of Lords *Hansard* shows only the most feeble attempts to impede or even reproach the government.

Another way in which some academics lent support to reduction was through their attitude to the humanities and social sciences, which were now under attack from government. In its extreme form, the need to put them in their place, and the new universities too, was expressed by Peter Dankwerts, professor of industrial chemistry at Cambridge, in a letter to *The Times* on 9 September 1981:

> During the period when the seaside universities were being set up, various technical colleges [such as Salford] were being upgraded to universities. But the staff and curriculum were not upgraded at the same time. They tended to ape Oxbridge by 'liberalising' their courses of studies. Why does Salford have a professor of contemporary history and politics?

The university study of engineering is intellectually demanding and very hard work. There is no room for woolly-mindedness. It is perhaps not surprising that there are more applicants for Eng lit than for engineering.

The 'seaside universities' presumably means Sussex which, in 1983-84 had 15 permanent (and three visiting) FRSs and one permanent (and two visiting) Nobel prize winners on its campus. English is a 'soft option', yet the Cambridge tripos traditionally allows very few 'firsts'. And all poor stylists and sloppy thinkers believe they are 'good at English'. Professor Dankwerts is ignorant of staffing changes that have taken place over the 17 or 18 years since the CATs received their charters. In both public and private sectors, some scientists and engineers regard the humanities as a soft option, and resent the apparently flexible and easy life style of the arts don.

The arguments for cutting the arts and social sciences were given quite briefly by the UGC in 1981: to make way for more scientists, engineers and others in 'useful' subjects. Yet, in fact, undergraduate recruitment to the 'hard' subjects has not been a success story; in 1972 over half of the unfilled places in universities (1,400 out of 2,744) were in engineering and technology, a matter which everybody concerned with the national well-being must regret. At the same time, however, science and engineering academics have felt themselves to be underprivileged. Yet their staffing ratios, equipment and buildings have always attracted far higher UGC allowances than those of the arts. In 1979-80 the gross cost per student in medical and related subjects was £6,535, in other science-based subjects £4,935, and in arts-based subjects £3,150.

Where does status lie in the British academic system? It is a myth to assume that the top of the system is inhabited by classics or other long-established arts subjects. Increasingly, the leadership roles are filled by scientists, technologists and medical professors. In 1981, of the 56 people reckoned by the CVCP to be of vice-chancellor status, only 19 came from an arts or social science background. Again, there are five research councils, and only one does not have a natural science base. By far the greater bulk of research council money goes to the natural sciences rather than the social sciences.* There is no

* The total budget for the five research councils was £463.9 million in 1981-82. Of this SERC received £234 million, MRC £107 million, ARC £86 million, NERC £56 million and SSRC £15 million (or less than 5 per cent of the whole).

humanities research council. The chairmanship of the UGC has been held by a chemist and an engineer on the last two occasions, and the latest appointee is a mathematician. Previously, the post was held by a succession of arts academics and then an economist. The Advisory Board for Research Councils which advises ministers on how to allocate money between different areas of research has always had a scientist as chairman. The top academics who receive the higher honours do so for one or two reasons. One is eminence in academic leadership or achievement; the other, increasingly adopted practice is to honour academics for obscure political purposes. By far the greatest number of peerages and knighthoods of the first kind go to academics in science, engineering and medicine.

Politicians accord great respect to science (which most of them do not understand) and less respect to those fields where they feel they may have something to contribute themselves – history or politics or literature. Moreover, the scientists themselves are remarkably confident at honouring their own colleagues and making their judgements stick in the public imagination. The Royal Society elects 40 fellows each year and thus confers distinction on a relatively large proportion of its own kind. The Society receives a grant of £4.5 million directly voted by parliament for the support of science. These enable the Royal Society to undertake many worthwhile national and international ventures. There is, however, no comparable system for adding distinction to one's own colleagues in the arts or social sciences, and a fellowship of the British Academy does not imply anything like a corresponding distinction.

During the period in which cuts were being imposed, the balance of power was decisively with the scientists. This is partly because of the in-built advantages in superior staffing ratios and heavy equipment and laboratories that science acquired during expansion, and partly because of the cultural and political preferences of the 1979-83 government.

Doubts and uncertainties leading to an inability to stand firmly by their institutions are to be expected from academics, who see too many sides of an argument too easily. It is difficult to imagine admirals defending a reduction of the navy or medical peers defending a reduction in expenditure on the NHS. Yet we were told of a very senior academic who indicated to a senior policy-maker that cuts would be acceptable as long as his own institution did not suffer unduly. Some vice-chancellors, consulted privately by politicians, did not resist notions of rationalisation. The Committee of Vice-

Chancellors and Principals, under the leadership of both Sir Alec Merrison and Dr Albert Sloman, protested vigorously and presented powerful arguments against the cuts in 1981 and earlier. Individual universities also protested strongly against the policy. But where were the leaders of the Oxford, Cambridge and London colleges or universities? Where they protested, they protested against certain biases in cuts, or the rate of change, or their own cuts. They did not step out of line to protect the weaker institutions. We have already quoted Parkes' account of the vice-chancellor who welcomed UGC interventions if they would help them strike out the departments which he regarded as being of low quality. The prevalence of these attitudes and divisions among academics meant that a government that had both narrow notions of social usefulness and narrow notions of academic excellence was not resisted by those with the status and prestige to put up effective opposition.

Finding a black sheep

Ministers have been equivocal about the reasons for reduction. Whilst they continue to claim that it was primarily expenditure-led, particular prejudices have certainly directed government policies. Yet if some 'hard' scientists were hostile to the humanities and social sciences, those scientists in positions of power within government advisory networks supported the social sciences when they were under attack and did not support Keith Joseph's attack on the SSRC. A letter to *The Times* on 24 February 1982 from Sir Robert Hinde, FRS, a leading biologist, pointed out that social sciences deal with subjects more complex and more difficult than landing a man on the moon or unravelling the structure of complex molecules. They are also relatively cheap.

But some academics in traditional subjects were uncertain about an expansion which brought so many social scientists in its wake. Social sciences, particularly sociology and some parts of psychology, seemed to be the hotbeds of radicalism. It was students, too, from the social sciences and to a lesser extent the humanities who broke the monopoly of teachers in the academic governance of universities – student membership of councils, senates and course boards was thrust upon unwilling academics at the end of the 1960s. In fact, those who led the troubles were not, in the view of many observers, the 'new' type of undergraduate but the essentially middle class, often public school, alienated and immature post-adolescents who would have entered university in earlier decades no matter how restricted the opportunities for the majority. We have been told of one large university where disciplinary action was being contemplated against students who led the disruptions. Recommendations to local authorities to stop their grants would have been of no avail because most were too rich to qualify for them.

In spite of remonstrances from those whom he most respected, a turning away from traditional standards of objectivity in policy-making for higher education is exemplified by the persecution of the social sciences by Sir Keith Joseph. In December 1981, he announced that he was inviting Lord Rothschild, a scientist turned banker and first head of the Central Policy Review Staff, to make an inquiry into the scale and nature of the SSRC's work.

Rothschild was asked to consider certain criticisms of sociology and of the SSRC. He considered whether it should be allowed to survive or whether its work should be handed over to other agencies; whether parts of the SSRC were unduly biased in favour of the unions; whether its judgement of research in economic and social history was poor; whether it was administratively inefficient; and whether the left-wing bias of the SSRC affected the objectivity of the research it sponsored. In his report Lord Rothschild referred to the unusual number of external inquiries during the last 10 years – about one a year on average – which had had a 'disequilibriating' effect. The SSRC's expenditure had been cut in real terms by 24 per cent in the last five years so that only the top echelons in social sciences could be supported. Postgraduate training awards had to be curtailed to a painful and undesirable extent and funds for this research were not available elsewhere.

Lord Rothschild concluded 'there is insufficient justification for saying that the SSRC and some of the social scientists it supports have any particular political ideology; and even if they had (and many of them must) there is no reason to assume that they would allow their political predilections to influence the conduct of their research.'[5] He recognised that social scientists had to deal with problems which have a political content. Yet he was naive enough to suggest that, because the SSRC's industrial relations unit at Warwick had been accused of being unfairly biased in favour of the unions, the chairman of the SSRC should 'set up an impartial examination to assess the complaint'. The report of the inquiry, led by Sir Kenneth Berrill, said that the accusation of bias 'has not been substantiated' and that 'the task of reducing the allegations from the level of generalisations to specific charges was a lengthy one.'[6]

This particular hare was set running by Lord Beloff in a question in the House of Lords in December 1981.[7] He suggested that 'there is in the academic community at large grave doubt about the efficiency and economy with which the Social Science Research Council has carried on its obligations', and he seemed concerned to advance the claims of the British Academy 'which does the same job for the humanities at very much less cost'. In fact, most humanities scholars would say that nobody performs this function adequately. Six months later Lord Beloff used parliamentary privilege to attack an academic by name:

> I note that of the two professors of education who are entrusted with important research functions by the Social Science Research Council at the moment, one is Professor Blackstone of the University of London, best known for her unremitting public assaults on selective and independent education. Many of us...concerned in the educational world, who have experience in it, would not regard research by Professor Blackstone as carrying with it the stamp of scholarly impartiality.[8]

Lord Beloff produced no evidence to show that Professor Blackstone had been other than scrupulously fair in her contributions to the decisions of the SSRC or the sub-committees and committees on which she serves. Using parliamentary privilege in this way is a betrayal of academic values. Academics have perfectly well-established ways of coping with bias. They publish, in as much detail and with as much venom as they like, their evaluation of other academics' work. But their attacks must be based on evidence and logic, not on personal bias or supposition. It is extraordinary that a person who has held the most senior political science post in Britain should make these kinds of attack. It is even more remarkable that Lord Rothschild should have taken them sufficiently seriously to suggest an inquiry into an academic group in a British university. Rothschild was reported to have said that when a Fellow of the British Academy makes such an accusation it must be taken seriously.

More recently, Sir Keith Joseph is reported to have enforced a change of name from 'Social Science Research Council' to 'Economic and Social Research Council', because he objected to the use of the word 'science'.[9]

The Conservative government had thus sponsored an atmosphere in which an underprivileged part of the academic system could be kicked hard at the same time as it was deprived of resources. Yet it can look for no protection from those academic barons who, though stoutly protesting their belief in excellence and academic values, are, in practice, among the first to diminish them.

Testing management skills

Vice-chancellors are almost all former professors, selected for both their academic standing and their ability to lead institutions. In the last few years, their qualities have been put under severe test. A university is not a simple managerial structure, but there are elements of hierarchy. For example, a lecturer is usually required to work 'under the direction of a head of department', but the same head of department and lecturer then meet on equal terms in a course board or some other committee where the more important policy decisions on curriculum and on distribution of resources are made. Even more fundamental is the fact that academic tenure has, in the past, conferred on each university teacher a 'freehold' – the term used for official fellowships in Cambridge colleges. A teacher cannot refuse to teach what is regarded as an essential element of a syllabus, but that syllabus will be decided collectively and not hierarchically, and the content and style of the teaching, and research, are largely impervious to scrutiny by colleagues.

The vice-chancellor is, therefore, required to preside over what is, in effect, a large college of academics rather than a hierarchical structure. At the same time, however, decisions have to be made about the allocation of resources, and, although these are made by committees, the shaping of the decisions is in the hands of the vice-chancellor. Moreover, he can vitally affect academic performance and behaviour because he is always present and has a *de facto* veto over appointments, promotions or developments that he thinks to be undesirable. Vice-chancellors can stop things expanding, but are able to do little once they are there. They cannot easily handle contraction, because previous decisions are set in bricks and mortar and in tenurial positions.

Given this fundamental dichotomy in university structure, how could a vice-chancellor suddenly be expected to handle reductions in resources that averaged 13 per cent? In many cases it might mean making scores of fellow academics redundant. Inevitably, there was tension within universities between those who had to manage the institution and those who formed parts of it. In the period of expansion universities had been selecting their members for life. Now the whole atmosphere changed. Vice-chancellors naturally wanted to ensure that the academics who went were those who were needed least.

The worst might not be the oldest, who could go with most money and least loss of self-esteem, but those who, perhaps appointed in their twenties or thirties a decade or so ago, had lost pace and commitment. The temptation to rectify previous mistakes must have been enormous.

Universities already feeling the pinch before the last round of cuts had to finance unmaintainable fixed assets against a potential decline in sponsorship by the UGC and student markets. Thus, London University possesses five major colleges and a larger number of smaller ones, each with some work of distinction but all ripe for 'rationalisation' in a world where saving resources is prized more than maintaining academic continuity. So the temptations within such a university must have been great to use the opportunity of cuts to impose major rationalisation.

Again, we have reports of some vice-chancellors welcoming the external pressure because it made it possible to get rid of second-rate academics and nuisances. At the same time, the call to reduce came in an unworkable form and over too short a period. As one vice-chancellor put it: 'If you ask me, do I have any staff I'd like to see the back of, of course I do, 2 or 3 per cent, but I have been asked to get rid of 7 to 8 per cent of people I don't want to get rid of'. So he chose to let buildings deteriorate because having a good staff would be an argument for improving the buildings later on.

If, however, managerialism, which is intrinsic to the role of a vice-chancellor, became sharpened by the requirements of government, others within the university felt that it was important to preserve existing conditions and relationships. There was indignation that tenures might be broken. There was anger at the wastefulness of paying colleagues large sums of money to stop doing useful work in order that fewer students might be educated and less research done. It was felt that academic life was undertaken by those who really wanted to do it, that those who have been recruited had forgone other opportunities, and that voluntary retirement, rather than compulsion, was essential.

So far, all heads of institutions have been compelled to adopt a policy of voluntary redundancy, though some have made tentative stabs at compulsion. Degrees of moral compulsion have been imposed. A teacher who is told that it would be better to go voluntarily, or the university will be compelled to go through the whole gamut of dismissal notice and court action and the like, is not really going voluntarily. Such conversations have taken place up and down

121

the country. As we have seen in one university (see Chapter 6), heads of departments declined to select their colleagues for such treatment and were put under notice of dismissal themselves. Elsewhere, heads of departments who shared the burden of vice-chancellors in having to be both managers over the smaller parts of institutions and senior members of the collegium found themselves dragged into negotiating voluntary severances. Goodwill and working efficiently achieved through mutual trust were lost in these transactions, which demanded instant assessments of previously free agents.

If most of those facing these problems deserve sympathy, some have found opportunity rather than disaster in the policies handed down to them. A vice-chancellor who is prepared to tell the chairman of the UGC in private that it is a pity that a department was not struck down by the UGC earlier seems to be flouting the ethics of decent behaviour. These demand that judgements result from open enquiry, open statement of fact and an opportunity for refutation. Others, because they genuinely believed that more meant worse, and were trying to build Harvards and MITs in unpromising places, were ambivalent in the face of the demands for contraction. Some were, indeed, overtly devoted to managerialism and took the opportunity to strengthen their position.

The notion of cutting out some staff and replacing them by others was not simply an idea held by ministers or die-hard science vice-chancellors as they approached the management of contraction. Some of the abler and more 'progressive' academics have remarked that the government could have produced useful results if it had only approached contraction properly. It could have got rid of some of the poorer academics recruited in the expansion which followed Robbins, and brought in new blood that would have benefited the system.

Where are our friends?
While the system responded too easily to the demands of government, higher education found itself remarkably short of friends. The specialist educational press, and above all, the *Times Higher Education Supplement*, gave sterling service to higher education, and to the wider community which never reads it, in monitoring the effects of the changes. The Association of University Teachers, always short of industrial muscle – for who cares if university teachers go on strike? – prepared itself as well as it could for real battles; successfully so in the cases of Aberdeen and Aston (see Chapter 6). The

parliamentary select committee specialising in education, under Christopher Price, interviewed those it felt were responsible for the new policies with great thoroughness. The TUC produced some ritual anguish. But none of those protests caused the government any discomfort. Higher education might, therefore, justifiably feel that it had no friends, and certainly no powerful lobby working on its behalf.

How did politicians react to the cuts? A few Conservative MPs criticised them. The opposition parties – Labour and the Liberal-SDP Alliance – did not grapple with the key issues of how to oppose the immediate reductions. The Labour Party had long been luke-warm in its defence of the universities, and ineffective in its resist-ance to cuts which were reducing the already limited opportunities. Some spokesmen, such as Phillip Whitehead, had a secure grasp of the damage being done and they began to be more effective in cross-examining ministers about the reduction of opportunity. But the party as a whole, as on so many detailed social policies, did not sum-mon its full force, and that of the trade unions and associated parts of the Labour movement, to counter them. The TUC and the National Executive Committee of the Labour Party called on the government to restore immediately the cuts in university spending. It was particularly opposed to the cuts in the technological universities, which had a higher working-class intake. The TUC was appalled that the allocations hit hardest five universities which placed great emphasis on the technological and science-based studies which were essential to the regeneration of British industry. It also accused the UGC of reinforcing the traditional hierarchy of British universities, and criticised its failure to reveal the criteria used.

By the time that the General Election of 1983 was announced Labour had clarified its policies for the future. In both *Education after 18: Expansion with Change* (February 1983) and its election manifesto, the party announced its determination to return to the Robbins principle of access to the willing and qualified and a restora-tion of £650 million over three years, but on conditions. Those univ-ersities which changed their ways to provide more open access would get the money and the others would be able to depend only on the 'rudiments of funding'.

The Liberal-SDP Alliance had also been critical of the policy, and Shirley Williams said that the UGC should have added quality and employability of students to its criteria. The Alliance manifesto promised to increase access. By contrast, the Conservative manifesto claimed that access by full-time students was now higher than under the last Labour government and that it was important for higher education 'to generate ideas and train the skilled workforce of the next generation. Within [the] budget, we want to see a shift towards technological, scientific and engineering courses'.[10]

The press was mixed in its responses to the cuts. Some papers rebuked the government, while others supported it. Eventually, some reaction set in against elements of government policy, particularly the increase in overseas student fees, but again criticism was muted, low-key and ineffective.

Despite some support from the opposition and the press, the universities felt themselves to be without friends. Higher education had not developed a lobby which was able to support it in its time of need. Lacking outside support academics were confused and uncertain about how to act. Many implicit doubts about the social objectives underlying expansion in the 1960s came to the surface, and 'new' subjects and the newer universities came under attack. The academic leadership proved inadequate in the face of a political challenge.

Many of the fundamental issues raised by the Conservative government's attack on the universities have never adequately been faced by our leading academics. For example, there is room for argument about how many young people and of what kind of ability should be admitted to undergraduate courses. Those who take the least liberal view of admission requirements have not squarely faced the relevant arguments. Are A levels a good indicator of potential ability? If there is doubt, why make it an indicator of institutional merit? How far can higher education institutions simultaneously cater for elites and for a somewhat wider but still highly selective group of the population without damage to the scientific work of the institutions? And, if elite professors and vice-chancellors feel that they themselves, or their institutions, should continue to cater for the small rather than the wider elite, what attitude should they take to the 'other' institutions when they are being attacked? What constitutes elite work? Is it not intellectually demanding to assess what knowledge will help solve the problems of inner city areas, or to train social workers, mental nurses, town planners or teachers? Must everything that is worth while within the academic world be related to the powerful paradigms of natural science or literary or historical scholarship? Does not good scholarship develop haphazardly, either from advances in theory or from the analysis of practical problems which lead on to ideas and theories?

Until issues such as these are faced, higher education will never be planned and developed in a way that reconciles its academic and social objectives. Academics must take responsibility for not having faced such central issues. And, because they had no philosophy with which to combat the government, they were weak, vacillating and divided in the face of an unexpected and wide-ranging attack. That had been, however, the licence granted them: to get on with their individual work and to be excellent. Could they not reasonably expect due notice before their terms of reference were changed?

References

1. Lord Flowers. Most recently at a conference organised jointly by the CBI and CVCP at Imperial College, London, November 1981
2. *THES*, 18 July 1975
3. A H Halsey, 'Quality and authority in British universities', *THES*, 1 March 1964. Survey repeated in 1974
4. House of Lords *Hansard*, debate on education expenditure cuts, 18 March 1981
5. House of Lords *Hansard*, 17 February 1972, pp 591-5
6. The Berrill report, Report of an Investigation into Certain Matters Arising from the Rothschild Report on the Social Science Research Council, May 1983, SSRC
7. House of Lords *Hansard*, question put by Lord Beloff, 15 December 1981, column 87
8. House of Lords *Hansard*, debate on Social Science Research Council, Rothschild report, 30 June 1982, columns 288-92
9. *THES*, 13 May 1983
10. *THES* and *Times Educational Supplement*, 20 May 1983

9. The Public Sector as Shock Absorber

This story has dealt mainly with the universities. That is partly because the government hit them hard and first and partly because its policies for the polytechnics and the rest of the public sector colleges are still, unpredictably and spasmodically, being developed.

A paradox in that policy is already clear. While the universities are supposedly 'private' institutions proudly brandishing their charters, the public sector* has, in fact, been able to protect itself to some extent because its funds do not come directly from the government but through local authorities. Public sector colleges can draw not only from the pool, over which the DES has control, but also from the rates which are not under direct government control. While the UGC can control university student numbers by imposing penalties on defaulters, the DES has not adopted powers to control student numbers in the public sector.

The universities were cut first and drastically. The public sector colleges were thus allowed to become the shock absorber for the whole higher education policy. They have, in the short run at least, been able to improve their standing, as abler students diverted from universities have filled up the many vacancies which they have always had. Those abler students, however, will find themselves in a sector whose standards of provision have never been generous and which will have deteriorated even more sharply than those of the universities.

The National Advisory Body for Local Authority Higher Education (NAB), which is apparently determined to establish higher academic standards and control over numbers in the public sector, can hardly fail to take a view on the extent to which public sector institutions should continue to act as an overflow for the universities. At the time, however, so eager have ministers been to claim that they have not reduced access to higher education that the

*There are also voluntary colleges, which receive grants directly from the DES.

DES has advised colleges and polytechnics, via NAB, that reduced staffing levels will be acceptable.[1] As we went to press there was growing anxiety among polytechnic directors about the unit of resource. The four college and polytechnic directors on NAB were voted down in their resistance to taking yet more students in 1984-85 despite a cut in income. One argued for delay in setting targets to allow planning in conjunction with the universities. This was not allowed.[2]

Growth of the public sector

Anthony Crosland believed that the polytechnics should compete with the universities. It was to be a parallel but equal system, a device so beloved by the British in their schools as well. It would scale its own heights, however, in the areas of applied knowledge, in taking more mature students, and in tapping industrial and public service needs.

Some of these aims have been achieved, although many universities were already undertaking, or have begun to perform, some of these functions. At the same time, the public sector institutions have been accused of aping the universities. Nevertheless, they have grown to form a resilient and widespread network able to accommodate the mature and part-time student unable to find a place in the predominantly residential universities. For many mature students, particularly those seeking part-time courses, public sector institutions have been the first rather than the second line of opportunity.

John Bevan, secretary of NAB, believes that politicians of all parties perceive higher education as taken full-time by 18-year-olds with A levels or the equivalent, 'and they don't always remember "or equivalent"'. The 18-plus A level holder is therefore a 'proxy' for everything else that goes on in higher education. Yet in the English local authority colleges there are over 300,000 students, of whom some two-thirds are mature. Of the full-time and sandwich course students, numbering well over 100,000, about a third are mature. If, then, funding arrangements are based on school-leaver figures, it is likely that a great deal of part-time work and work for mature entrants will be reduced unthinkingly at the same time as Sir Keith Joseph restricts opportunity for school-leavers.

Within this public provision the Robbins principle of meeting all qualified demand had been sustained. The expansion of teacher training helped to secure this policy. In the early 1960s there were only 24,000 teacher training places. This was rapidly increased to over 130,000 but then reduced again – to 38,000 by 1981-82. Teacher training is the best illustration of how fine-tuning of higher education to meet specific manpower demands can fail. Yet the present government is continuing to make the same kind of planning assumption about information technology, irrespective of whether there is the manpower and demand to sustain a £350 million development and research programme.

By the time that different demographic projections had been absorbed into the planning system, 12 colleges of education had been merged with universities, 37 with polytechnics, 24 with colleges of further education, and 26 with other colleges of education; 27 remained as independent colleges, 25 had closed, and one had ceased all kinds of teacher training. In 1981 not one of the former colleges of education offered the same courses it had provided in 1972. This reorganisation produced 67 institutions describing themselves as colleges of higher education. They formed, in effect, a third kind of higher education institution outside the universities and polytechnics.

Many students who would have taken a teacher training course would now find a place on another course. But we have already seen how the opportunities for women in particular were reduced, or at least women failed to take up places in line with the general trend, because places previously held in women's teacher training colleges were now converted to general and co-educational purposes. The present cuts in arts and social sciences are likely further to reinforce the balance against higher education for women.

Government uncertainties

After the creation of the binary system in 1965 the public sector grew rapidly, and developed more or less in response to student and local demand. By the late 1970s many observers thought that a period of rationalisation, on academic as much as on financial grounds, was overdue if students were not to be poorly served as reductions in spending took effect.

But in making cuts in the public sector, the government has been inconsistent. It has treated it differently from the universities by allowing it to take more rather than fewer students and has thus, virtually by stealth, moved the line dividing the two systems.

In the 1980 Education Act the DES set an annual limit on the amount of expenditure on higher education which LEAs could pool. This 'capping of the pool' meant that local authorities could no longer continue to expand public sector provision so freely. The criteria for the approval of courses were tightened up. Approvals were placed within a more restrictive framework. Courses would only be approved if they met the needs of industry for skilled technological or scientific workers or were essential to regional or national employment; if they were replacing, with only minor modifications, existing advanced full-time and sandwich courses; or if they were financed by outside sponsors.

The wish to bring the sector under control was also reflected in the 1978 Oakes Brown Paper, the Green Paper of the same year, which suggested different modes of governance including one depriving local authorities of control,[3] and the creation of NAB. In 1980 the DES devised a form of manpower planning known as the 'broad steer'. There was to be central direction of the numbers in broad subject groupings, but this model of planning was not adopted by the incoming Conservative government in 1979. Instead, it set up NAB which would make judgements based on evaluations of institutions within a policy of financial constraint.

Between 1979 and 1981 the DES and local education authorities wrestled with the question of how expenditure on public higher education would be controlled and by whom. It was decided that a committee of the National Advisory Body, chaired by the minister responsible for higher education, would determine academic provision in certain fields and give approval to advanced courses. The new interim body was announced on 23 December 1981. At about the same time the announcement of a 'capped pool' of £539 million meant a cut of some 6.5 per cent between 1980-81 and 1982-83, with a reduction of 2,000 teaching staff in each of the next two years and corresponding non-teaching cost cuts.

The 1982-83 Expenditure White Paper announced a 10 per cent cut in expenditure by 1983-84. The cuts were to be worked through at the same time as the National Advisory Body was to set to work on a more radical plan for rationalisation.

The cuts must be considered against those imposed on the universities. The universities were cut because the country 'could not afford' to keep them at their existing size, and 18,000 places were taken out during the peak years for the recruitment age group and at a time when the age participation rate was beginning to pick up.

Inevitably, students began to flood into the polytechnics. In 1981-82 the age participation rate* was 13.2 per cent – 5 per cent higher

* See note on page 25 for the DES recalculation of APR.

than in the previous year. The universities' share, however, fell from 7.5 to 7.2 per cent, and the public sector share increased from 5.2 to 6 per cent. Part of the thinking of the elite academics was thus met by a transfer of students, including some with three Cs, from the university sector to the public sector. At the end of 1982, Bristol Polytechnic had an increase of 80 per cent in applications on the previous year, while the Polytechnic of Central London estimated a 120 per cent increase. The business studies department at Oxford Polytechnic received 1,020 applications for 50 places. It could, in 1982, have had a first-year intake composed entirely of students with two grade Bs at A level.

The universities had had to restrict their intakes, ostensibly to preserve the 'unit of resource', but also, it has been inferred, to save student awards. Some of those which exceeded the UGC limits have been fined. Would not the same policy apply to the polytechnics and other public sector colleges? The 1982 Expenditure White Paper confirmed a reduction of 10 per cent in real terms between 1980-81 and 1984-85, which would mean a loss of one in six teaching posts. But when NAB met in February 1981 it found that the DES was allowing for a substantial increase in student numbers in colleges and polytechnics at the cost of higher staff/student ratios and a reduced unit of resource. This was in stark contrast to the plans for the universities.

The DES paper conceded that in order to take the greater number of students anticipated, a 10 per cent target reduction would be tough for the colleges, but no attempt was made to find more money. The DES offered the view that an overall staff/student ratio of 12:1 ought to be feasible by a selective increase in non-science subjects. In the sciences, the ratio would be 10.6:1 while others would rise by 39 per cent to 14.5:1.

The public institutions thus had to face the unexpected and implicit connivance of the DES – but not all were willing anyway – in increasing student numbers, while having a serious cut in resources. NAB's secretariat estimated that government and local authority cuts would result in overall budget reductions of about 15 per cent, which should have meant halving the number of students admitted in that year or spending 20 per cent less per student. But it was apparently the DES's view that performance and class size were not related; an assumption mysteriously not applied to universities by the UGC.

Student grants, though administered by LEAs, are paid for largely by central government. But it has no power to instruct local authorities to withhold grants once a student has been given a place, and cannot control the numbers admitted. The vice-chancellors' fears were thus realised. The universities lost student numbers as well as money. The large increase in numbers in the peak years would be accommodated more cheaply in the public sector, irrespective of the danger that a loss of students would bring to the universities. Both sides of higher education would lose staff in roughly the same proportions. But it is obvious that institutions which are able to retain student numbers can also retain courses. The option to stretch resources for a while until the peak had passed was not given to the universities.

The government's policy for public sector higher education can be criticised on two grounds. First, the policy was not adequately co-ordinated with the cuts in university education. There was serious injustice across the binary divide, and inevitably good courses in universities will be closed while less good ones in the public sector will be retained, though with fewer resources. The government operated its policies through two different sets of financial machinery, which it was in its power to modify. Because it could not control one sector as easily as the other, it allowed the machinery to determine the policy, irrespective of the educational and institutional impact.

Second, in a country which is largely under-educated, money cutbacks in the public sector (whose unit costs are already lower than those of the universities), at a time when its resource base should have been expanding and adapting itself more to the needs of mature students, part-time students and disadvantaged groups with particular needs, such as ethnic minorities, demonstrate the government's negligence of its duty to provide a 'comprehensive education system for the population of England and Wales'. These words appeared in the 1944 Education Act, drafted by a Conservative statesman, R A Butler, but they were ignored in both spirit and letter by the 1979-83 government.

The National Advisory Body has the daunting task of rationalising provision, within a framework of severe cuts, in over 400 institutions in England and Wales. The criteria are now being made explicit, and the evaluation, which is likely to depend on such outside sources as the CNAA's subject committees, will be competent. But we must be tempted to paraphrase Edward Parkes' statement to both the Secretary of State and the select committee: government can cut higher education if it thinks the country cannot afford it and can finish up with any kind of higher education system that it wants. It seems extraordinary, however, that decisions affecting the education of nearly 600,000 full-time students, an even greater number of part-time students and 50,000 teachers should be taken in so unco-ordinated a fashion that the ultimate pattern promises to be hap-hazard, wasteful and arbitrary. The government was not concerned about the impact on people or on institutions, but only about the relatively minor sums, compared with expenditure in areas of other public activity, which it might save by these efforts.

Ultimately, the binary system will have to go. Those who teach young people in schools or higher education know how arbitrary and fractional differences in quality are at the borderline. No academic can defend the differences in treatment given to one student with three Cs and another with two Cs and a D. Examination perform-ance can leap by two or three grades within three or four months on a retake. Those who teach in the less prestigious universities are quite used to the phenomenon of the 'fractured profile' – a student with perhaps an A, a C and an E who has been refused admission to some other university because he has not met the terms of his conditional offer, but who, with sympathetic tutoring, can fulfil his potential. But, while those clever or lucky enough to attend the well-established universities enjoy good libraries and well-established residential and communal facilities, their contemporaries or those returning to education after a period of work or child-bearing, may find them-selves in poorly funded institutions, with virtually no library facili-ties and no tutorial system.

At a time of radical contraction and reorganisation, these issues could have been discussed openly. But that would have required care and thought and knowledge. Instead, a haphazard, sloppy and uncaring scheme for contraction administered across an artificial institutional divide has meant that the worst will get worse and the best will be reduced in self-confidence and resources. The public sec-tor will act as the dumping ground for a generation of newly down-graded students, who were thought to be also-rans by the political and academic leadership, but are nonetheless among the most highly qualified of the present generation.

References

1. NAB 21/83, paper by DES, 'Implications of the Government's Expenditure Plans for Local Authority Advanced Further Education'

2. *THES*, 13 May 1983
3. DES, Report of the Working Group on the Management of Higher ·
   Education in the Maintained Sector, Cmnd 7130, March 1978

10. Losing a Generation

Higher education is at the mercy of three major external factors: population changes – the number of children born each year who eventually become part of the pool from which higher education students are recruited; the decisions of policy-makers on how many places to provide and for what proportions of each age group; and the motivation of young people to compete for higher education courses.

Many countries have experienced major problems caused by fluctuations in the birth rate. Britain, in common with every other European country, has experienced troughs and bulges in age groups, and these have played havoc with educational planning. Educational institutions of all types have had to alternate between overcrowding and empty places. But at least policy-led demography was a constant factor after the Robbins report was accepted in 1963. Its fundamental precept was that 'courses of higher education should be made available to all those who are qualified by ability and attainment to pursue them and wish to do so', even if government could vary the way in which that principle of access should be applied.

For example, in the 1960s a large number of places became available for those who wished to pursue teacher training. Until the early 1960s there were about 24,000 teacher training places. These reached a peak of 130,000 places by the end of the 1960s to accommodate the extra students produced by the increase in the length of the training course, and to prepare for the anticipated increase in demand for teachers. But recent government policy has now reduced the number to less than 38,000.

Declining demand for places
It was not changes in policy but an apparent reduction in demand that first caused expansion to slow down and then stop. The figures must be used with caution. The proportion of the age group recruited reached a peak of 14.2 per cent in 1972. But that figure included teacher trainees with less than two A levels. If they are left out, there

was a peak of just under 12 per cent in 1978, then a relatively stable state and an increase by 1982-83 to 13.2 per cent.[1] The qualified participation rate (QPR) has also begun to climb because of the increased recruitment in the public sector. But these relatively stable rates, and small peaks, should not conceal the fact that the objective had been an APR of 22 per cent. This was never reached. Government policy could have stimulated continued expansion by encouraging young people to stay in school, and older people and underrepresented groups, such as women and ethnic minorities to take some form of higher education.

There are many explanations for the slowing down of demand. Young people may have become disenchanted with education, perhaps as a result of the growing conviction that higher education did not necessarily lead to high-status employment. Moreover, inflation and pay policy in the mid-1970s 'pressed hard on people in the kind of occupations graduates normally enter ... and it looked as if employment prospects were deteriorating'. A further reason produced by Toni Griffiths is that students might have had their own conception of 'rate of return'.[2] The ratio of student grants to the retail price index showed that students' standard of living fell sharply after the middle 1970s.

The slackening home demand was initially made up by students from overseas, the number of which rose from 31,000 in 1967-68 to 85,000 in 1979. But the number of new overseas postgraduate entrants then fell by 23 per cent between 1978 and 1980-81 and undergraduates by 29 per cent between 1977 and 1980-81.

Another reason for weaker home demand is the confused state of education for 16- to 19-year-olds. Local authorities and schools have had to provide adequate post-16 education at a time of financial pressure and while the school population has been falling. The percentage of those staying on after 16 is low among some social groups. While nearly one in three stayed in English schools after 16, there were large differences between pupils at independent schools (71.5 per cent of whom stayed on for two years) and maintained schools (26 per cent, mainly for one year), and between boys and girls and different regions of the country.[3]

Local authorities have found it difficult, indeed in many areas, impossible, to create viable sixth forms or new tertiary colleges (combining sixth form study and further education) with a good range of courses. Many local authorities have had to produce makeshift arrangements. Moreover, some attempts by local authorities to

THE ATTACK ON HIGHER EDUCATION

provide viable systems have been forbidden by ministers anxious to preserve traditional patterns of schooling. Many maintained schools have had to choose between helping the least able and most disadvantaged and pushing their abler pupils to greater heights.

A higher education system can only work properly if a strong demand for it is created by adolescents whose school experiences have given them an appetite for more education. Slackening demand for higher education reflects on the failure of the political, administrative and professional leadership of those responsible for offering provision for A level work. It also reflects on the failure of higher education to mesh more closely with the schools and to show itself to be accessible to all groups. It may also reflect on the schools' approach to the task of encouraging the learning skills and academic appetites of young people.

Student finance, too, is an important factor. Once they have made the grade and secured places in higher education, young people receive awards enabling those from low-income families to take up courses. Local authority provision varies for the 16- to 19-year-olds. Those from low-income families have to choose between remaining a burden on their families or seeking employment at 16. Class differentiation is strikingly apparent in the staying on rates after 16. Thus the country loses some of its ablest young people because it may not fund them in these vital years of transition from school to higher education. Because of the lack of state support or encouragement, we have a low staying-on rate compared with most Western countries.

Changing patterns of demand

In response to Robbins the government had accepted targets up to 1973 – a 10-year span – and had allowed funds to the UGC, including £650 million for capital expenditure, for the purpose of funding expansion. Yet the Robbins projections actually seemed to underestimate the demand. The proportion obtaining two or more A levels rose from 6.9 per cent in 1961 to 9.6 per cent in 1966, compared with Robbins' estimate of 8.4 per cent. Student numbers went up in every area except that of overseas students, where the proportion of the total fell. In 1970 the DES was forecasting 835,000 full-time students by 1981. Furthermore, the establishment of the Open University in 1971 led to the registration of 40,000 students by 1977 and 60,000 by 1980.

In the 1972 White Paper the DES revised the figure, and projected that 22 per cent of the age group would occupy 750,000 higher education places in 1981 as against the earlier figure of 835,000. It was intended that students be shared equally between the universities and the public sector institutions, against the advice of Robbins' report which gave pre-eminence to the universities. From then on the target figures were successively reduced. In 1974 the target for 1981 was cut to 650,000; in 1976 to 600,000 even though this implied an increase in the competition for entry in some places; in 1977 to 560,000 by 1981-82 the figure said by Robbins to be 'conservative'.[3] In 1977 the government decided that the universities were to increase to 310,000 places rather than 290,000, and the non-university institutions were to stay at 250,000 by 1981. Parity had been assumed in the 1972 White Paper. But the birth rate fell from 1964 to 1977, although the percentage of 18-year-olds throughout the 1970s leaving school with two A levels steadily rose.

By the time the latest and most drastic cuts began to be felt in the autumn of 1981, the home student age participation rate stood at 12.9 per cent. There were 535,000 full-time and sandwich students in higher education, the highest number ever. In that year, the number of first year home students increased by a total of 5 per cent. The increase was accommodated mainly by the advanced further education sector (polytechnics and colleges), which went up by 13 per cent. The number of first year students in universities fell by 3 per cent, although the number of applications increased by 4 per cent. It was also a year when the expansion of the previous decade bore fruit: 23 per cent more first degrees were awarded in 1980 than in 1976, and this included a 52 per cent increase in degrees awarded by the CNAA. By contrast, in 1980-81 overseas student numbers fell by 9 per cent, and now comprised only 9 per cent of total student numbers, compared with 11 per cent in 1976-77.

Further important changes are concealed in these figures. In 1981-82 42.7 per cent of home students were women, slightly more than in 1980-81 and other recent years but less than in 1976-77 when there were far more students on teacher training courses. The *DES Bulletin* containing these figures states: 'It seems likely that the percentage of all home students who are women may level out for a time at [42.9 per cent], which is the percentage of first-year women students.'[4] About 23.5 per cent of home entrants to full-time courses were mature entrants (ie aged 21 or over), a slightly higher percentage than in the previous year but a reduction from a year earlier. It is likely that mature people would hesitate to enter full-time courses because they were keen to retain their existing employment.

137

As pupils move from sixth forms to higher education, the class divide widens. In spite of the social advances since the Second World War, social classes A and B still provide quite disproportionate numbers of students in sixth forms and at university.[5] There are no analogous figures for the public sector. These classes occupied only 23 per cent of the places at age 16, but this rose to 60 per cent at age 18. At university, entrants with fathers in social classes A and B increased from 44 per cent to 51 per cent between 1970 and 1975. The proportion of students from working-class homes fell between 1956 and 1980. There were also astonishing regional disparities. 'University participation rates in Scotland are 26 per cent above the English and Welsh average, whereas for the contiguous north of England region they are 21 per cent below.'[6]

If the schools have failed to retain, and higher education to recruit, whole groups of the population who could benefit from it, teachers in comprehensive schools are certainly aware of able young people, particularly girls, with no tradition of higher education in their families, who leave at 16 despite their A level and degree potential. Many who leave at 16 regret it later, and the last two decades has seen a significant rise in the number of part-time courses. For the number of part-time students grew by 75 per cent in the 1970s compared with a growth rate of only 11 per cent in the number of full-time students. The total number of both full- and part-time home students was 749,300 in 1980-81, an increase of 29 per cent over the 10 years.

At a time when demand for places is up and when there are untapped demands from under-recruited social groups, a greater number of places are being cut in the universities than ever before. By June 1982 nearly 250 university courses had been closed. In October 1981, although there was a 4 per cent increase in applications to universities, the number admitted was 3,200 (3 per cent down on the previous year). The average A level 'score' of entrants rose from 9.1 to 10.1 points (an A grade counts as 5 and an E grade 1). The University Central Council on Admissions said that there appeared to have been an appreciable increase in the number of apparently well-qualified candidates who failed to gain admission to university in 1981. Demand for university places increased by a further 4 per cent in 1982.

It is difficult to use government figures to calculate the number of school-leavers deprived of university places. We have Parkes' figure of the universities taking only 60 per cent of those willing and qualified to enter university. And we have the official estimates of losses between 1982 and 1985, given in a parliamentary answer by William Waldegrave on 16 March 1982: 'The number of additional . . . students who would have to be admitted . . . to match the proportion . . . admitted in 1980-81 would be: 15,000 in 1982-83, 21,000 in 1983-84 and 25,000 in 1984-85.' So some 61,000 young people will fail to secure places in the four years from the autumn of 1980.

The government, having failed to control local authorities, has allowed some of these losses to be taken up by the public sector. But we cannot be sure how far, and for how long, the losses of university places will be cushioned by allowing the public sector institutions to increase their numbers.

At the end of 1981 the government announced that the money available for non-university higher education provided by local authorities would be cut by about 6.5 per cent between 1980-81 and 1982-83. This would mean a loss of 2,000 teaching staff in each of the next two years and corresponding reductions in non-teaching costs. It was generally assumed that this would mean a cut in student numbers – to meet the Boyson-style of argument which questioned the numbers receiving higher education, to retain parity of treatment with that meted out to universities, and because the public sector could not sustain such financial losses without either losing student places or allowing serious deterioration in staffing standards. But the government has failed to stop public sector institutions increasing their numbers, regardless of reduced money and staffing, to take the increased demand.

Estimates of places lost must thus be hazardous. The continuing lack of employment opportunities for young people will sustain pressure from qualified entrants to higher education. Unemployment among older people may cause them to seek higher education. The social class factor – a higher birth rate among the A and B groups – will ensure that the pool of applicants falls less than the proportion of the total age group. Moreover, some local authorities are making determined efforts to increase opportunities for women and persuading girls to stay at school beyond the age of 16. On the supply side, if we assume that NAB rationalisation takes place, and if the government does not continue to use the public sector as the parking lot for all who have failed to secure places at the university, perhaps a further 80,000 qualified students will fail to secure a place in higher education from the mid-1980s until the mid-1990s. This is in addition to the 60,000 denied a place in the period 1982-85.

At the time it made the cuts the government made no public prediction of what the pattern of lost opportunity would be. It may well be that it will change the patterns of permitted recruitment from year to year in the face of actual demand. Political pressure, too, may force a change of plan. The government has not been able to hold down public sector numbers in the coming year and has, through NAB, virtually imposed further increases for 1984-85, although it has drastically cut the pool of resources. But allowing the public sector to take more students does nothing to meet increased demand for part-time courses.

Recently, the government attempted to predict future demand for places. It now expected higher education to enrol considerably more students than when it made its last formal projection of demand in 1979. The APR will rise steadily from 13.5 per cent to between 14.9 and 15.9 per cent in the 1990s. It also admitted that 'if the number of places currently available were to be maintained, the supply of places currently available would, sooner or later, exceed demand.' The reasons for this prediction, which reads so bizarrely against the recent cuts in university places, are that the qualified recruitment rate has increased from 85 to 88 per cent since 1979 and that unemployment will increase demand from qualified young, if not from older people.[7]

Even these figures, which imply a U-turn in thinking, have been criticised as too conservative. The Principal of Edinburgh University pointed out that while the figures took account of the higher middle class birth rate, they ignored the steady increase of recruitment of women.[8]

The 1979-83 government made a radical break with the post-war consensus on educational policy. Ministers are said to be working on yet even more far-reaching changes all likely further to undermine the system. The introduction of student loans, reported to be occupying Sir Keith Joseph's mind, but then suddenly abandoned, would add to the disincentives to poor students, but make it cheaper for the families of the rich to finance their children's higher education, as has happened in the USA. The Central Policy Review Staff produced a document in September 1982 which was immediately leaked to *The Economist*. It proposed the privatisation of all higher education – in universities, polytechnics and colleges – and an end of their state funding. It was alleged to have proposed full-cost tuition fees of at least £4,000 a year. There would be 300,000 means-tested scholarships for the brighter students (as opposed to the

560,000 local authority awards now made), and the others would be eligible for loans. This might, said the report, save £1,000 million a year.

Attitudes in the schools
What effect have the policies we have criticised had on the expectations of young people? Anybody who has contact with 16-year-olds will know that many now fear unemployment. Any place lost in higher education is likely to create, through a knock-on effect, a corresponding place in the dole queue. Savings in student awards, which are also beyond government control, are largely offset by the costs of increased supplementary and unemployment benefits.

Part of the motivation to write this book came from a conversation with the head of a school who had found that five sixth formers who, in her opinion, should certainly have entered higher education, had either failed to get places, because entry qualifications were made higher, or who had dropped out because of disenchantment with their chances.

We attempted to make a closer study of this matter by inviting heads of schools and colleges in the inner London area to complete a questionnaire showing the changes that expectations of cuts had made on young people. We were told that if our questionnaires had been sent out a year later it is likely that the full effects would have worked their way through to affect more strongly young people's and the schools' knowledge of the consequences. We have no way of knowing what biases are reflected in the voluntary sample of those who replied. But the responses contain interesting comments which touch on our analysis.

In the 42 schools and colleges which returned our questionnaire, only 26 per cent of the 4,338 sixth formers (or their equivalents in colleges) entered for two A levels or more in 1981. Of these, only 40 per cent (440) went on to higher education. According to their teachers' responses, 4.5 per cent of those taking two A levels or more would have secured places in previous years but did not do so. And, significantly, about 12 per cent of the sixth formers who failed to get places would, in the opinion of their teachers, have benefited from higher education.

A majority of, but not all, respondents believed that the standards required for admission had changed in 1982. One school noted that scientists and mathematicians could have gained entry with two Es say, eight years ago, but that better grades, particularly in science,

141

were now essential to gain conditional UCCA acceptances. Some subjects, such as accounting, business studies, some of the sciences and maths, had definitely increased their demands. To some it seemed difficult in 1982 to obtain a place in a university with less than C grades. It was suggested that universities were less willing to accept students who did not get the precise grades specified in conditional offers. The 'points' system (whereby, for example, a student failing to get three Cs might be accepted on a B, C and a D) seemed to have been abandoned by some. One school noted roughly a grade increase in demands.

These are not surprising conclusions. As the cuts become sharper, these trends will become more observable to all schools. There were some exceptions: one college noticed that there was more, rather than less, flexibility in favour of their mature students.

The replies revealed what psychological impact the cuts and the general economic climate had had on young people. We asked our respondents whether they noticed any decline in the number of pupils applying for higher education or for courses leading to higher education because they assumed that it would be more difficult to secure admission. One of the most successful schools in London at securing places replied that some sixth formers now expect to need higher grades than they feel they can achieve, even when there has been no increase in standards.

One large comprehensive had not noticed a decline in pupil expectations, but had passed on to students information about the cutbacks in higher education and the fact that universities and polytechnics were much less flexible than they used to be in allowing people in 'under the net'. 'To this extent, we have contributed to a change in expectation. No decrease in numbers coming forward noted, but a less optimistic attitude is noticeable.' It was in that school that nine students failed to gain entry because the competition for places in a particular field was strong, enabling the university or polytechnic to maintain a standard offer which the students failed to achieve. 'The pity is that appropriate higher education is not available for all those who want or need it and qualify.' In another school the reply was that 'there is always a problem . . . because most of our girls enter as first-generation higher education students, sometimes still against parental opposition. More of the very bright girls are questioning whether to go on, but this is the unemployment factor rather than cutbacks on higher education. There seems to be an increase in anxiety which is curtailing social development.'

The schools reflect the paradoxical responses of young people, who find it increasingly difficult to know how to play their chances in a harsher market. One school noticed a trend for pupils securing five O levels to consider employment rather than as in past years to continue almost automatically to A level. In another school, some able pupils left at 18 or even 16 because they felt a job in a bank or the civil service is best seized when available. 'They all tell of unemployed graduates they know.' Another school thought that higher education had become more attractive because of fears of unemployment.

Elsewhere, pupils chose further education at 16-plus, and thus reduced the size of sixth forms. Sometimes the temptation of receiving £25 a week on YOP and CEP schemes proved a disincentive to study. One school implied that cuts produced positive advantages because students were more questioning about the realities, and looked at a wider range of institutions. They became more keenly aware of the need to achieve higher grades and more realistic about themselves. Another felt that the difficulty was to discourage them from entering higher education. Many more students were hedging their bets by applying to polytechnics as well as to universities.

The general impression is that expectations have been reduced, and that pupils who could have benefited from higher education are instead looking for jobs as a source of instant security. On the plus side, some of the more unrealistic expectations have been exposed and school-leavers now look at a wider range of institutions. But the bleakest conclusion is that many young people now seem to be influenced by the twin fears of failing to get into higher education or failing to get a job if they do succeed in taking a degree course.

We asked for other evidence to help us assess the impact of reductions on the work of sixth forms and the opportunities for young people in them. Vocational courses were becoming more popular. Teachers felt that pupils' anxiety was restricting their development. Young people were looking very carefully for advanced level courses which were 'career-directed' rather than continuing the subjects which they enjoyed at school. Another school noticed the disappearance of some joint degree courses. Others pointed to the growing disincentives to study: 'the thought that three years' study would be followed by unemployment was a powerful factor in dissuading some young people from applying.'

Another head suggested, after conversations with admission tutors and other university staff, that the impact on sixth form work had not yet been felt. It was more likely to make an impact in two to

143

three years' time. Problems of rivalry between departments in universities for resources had been alluded to three times in such conversations. 'The level of stress in the second-year sixth has risen among those applying to university.' Another sixth form head noted the peculiar difficulties 'of this very difficult inner city school [which] do undoubtedly produce lower standards of A level grades. Although the specific problems are carefully explained in my references to the polytechnics and UCCA, little notice seems to be taken since the performance grades required appear not to be reduced.'

These responses suggest that while a minority of schools seem to welcome a new realism among their pupils, the majority have noticed wasted opportunities, a growth of anxiety, and some distortion of the objectives of sixth form education. The problems now being induced in British education are well typified by one comment: 'An extremely well-qualified and able young man was not even invited to interview when applying for medicine. This resulted in a complete breakdown on his part.'

The government was concerned to save money. It accepted the UGC's assumption that it should cut opportunity for young people rather than 'excellence' and research capacity. The cost to the country – in terms of the frustrated ambitions of young people at a time of high and rising unemployment, and the loss of enhanced skills – did not enter the calculation.

References

1. DES Report on Education No 99, Future Demand for Higher Education in Great Britain, April 1983
2. T Griffiths, 'The development of higher education since the Robbins report', Appendix A to G Williams and T Blackstone, *Excellence in Diversity*, Society for Research in Higher Education, 1983
3. DES, Statistics of Education, HMSO 1981
4. Griffiths, op cit and DES *Statistical Bulletin* 9/82, October 1982, Higher Education in Great Britain: Funding Figures for 1981/82
5. DES *Statistical Bulletin*, op cit
6. DES Report on Education No 86, G Williams, A Gordon and the Office of Population, Censuses and Statistics
7. DES Report on Education No 99, op cit
8. *THES*, 6 May 1983

11. A Cause for Public Concern

This book presents an unedifying picture of government policy. That policy was designed to save money by cutting institutions which both advanced knowledge and provided opportunities for young people, whose recruitment numbers were at a peak at the time when the cuts were imposed. The government's own guilt about the effects of its policy is displayed in the later retractions which not only confirmed the wrongness of its original judgements, but also revealed the biases and predispositions underlying the original policy.

The attack launched in 1980 on higher education through the imposition of full fees on overseas students has been modified by the increase of £46 million in aid over three years to help foreign students in Britain. The cutback in finance for foreign students had, according to the *Guardian*, been widely criticised in the Foreign Office. Ministers and officials travelling abroad are reported to have encountered bad feeling among friendly countries because of its effects. But whereas in the past universities have been free to accept students from any country, the new policy will benefit students from immediate British dependencies such as Hong Kong, or countries such as Malaysia with which the UK government is anxious to maintain good relations.

This revised policy does not break down the little Englandism of the original policy, but merely extends the boundaries of Little England. In principle, education should have no national boundaries. The damage to Britain's status and ability to sell abroad caused by the original policy to save money is incalculable. The revised policy subordinates higher education to foreign policy.

The second retraction of policy concerns the recruitment of 'new blood'. The government is providing the UGC with funds earmarked for 230 lecturers, of whom 30 will be in the arts and social sciences. Similar numbers will be allowed in later years. More than 2,000 applications have been received by the University Grants Committee, mostly for multi-disciplinary research of a strongly practical nature in areas such as operations research and biochemical genetics.

145

The UGC and research councils will choose the subjects in which universities may appoint these teachers; they are to spend most of their time on research and must be under 35. The government's speedy decision to restore this number of posts confirms our contention that the cuts were not purely 'expenditure-led'. There is still money available. The cuts were converted into a process of culling, particularly in social sciences and humanities teaching, in order to make way for items on ministers' academic, work-related shopping list. Of these, the enthusiasm of the 1979-83 government for information technology was a prime example. The provision of university teaching and research posts was part of a £350 million research programme, including £300 million for industrial research. Academics in the field feared that the demands to be made on the small group of academics would be too great.[1]

The divergence of policy between the universities and the public sector also represents a retraction. The government intended to reduce both sectors, but found it could not stop students applying for and receiving local authority grants once they were accepted in the public sector, and that it could not control the numbers of students accepted by the polytechnics and colleges. If Rhodes Boyson was right – that too many were taking degree courses – the government should have imposed new controls enabling it to forbid polytechnics taking as many students as in previous years. Yet they took more. In Boyson's universe, there would have been a kind of bastardised parity of esteem between the universities and the polytechnics, because both would enjoy teaching more rigorously selected students. But in the absence of such controls the universities are being punished for taking more students than the UGC limit, while the institutions supposedly under stronger public control are increasing their numbers and retaining departments which, had they been in universities, might have been closed.

Universities have been pressed into setting higher admission standards. Students capable of securing second class degrees from universities will not have that option, but will find themselves in institutions not among their first group of preferences. This not only impairs the freedom of the universities to take the range of ability which they feel they can enhance, but also attacks one of the assumptions of public sector policy. Public institutions were intended to eschew academicism and to be concerned with the renewal of opportunity and the recruitment of a wide range of students. But now the premium is being raised as 18-year-old students with three Cs or even two Bs compete for places in some polytechnics. The temptation for them to become even more like universities, favouring the bright school-leavers, will be reinforced. But for how long we cannot tell. We do not know whether the public sector's reprieve is temporary or not. We do not know how long they can last on the severely reduced resources with which they must cope with increased numbers.

So, again, the government's nonchalant disengagement from the consequences of its actions is shown to be false. It gave ground on its original policy so that it might accommodate the peak numbers of young people entering higher education in 1983. Its acceptance of the fact that the polytechnics might accept the increased numbers was slipped in quite late in the whole planning process – at a meeting of the National Advisory Body held in March 1983.

The inconsistency and bias of government are demonstrated clearly by its treatment of the University College of Buckingham. The *THES* pointed out that the New University of Ulster was being forced to merge with a polytechnic and would lose its charter because it was 'too small'. Yet it has 1,700 full-time students and a good range of subjects with the exception of engineering. By contrast, the University College of Buckingham, founded by Lord Beloff to advance the cause of private university education, has 470 students, more than half from overseas, concentrates on four teaching subjects and its 'commitment to research is vestigial'. But Buckingham secured from Conservative ministers an agreement that its students would be eligible for local authority awards, including a contribution towards tuition fees, and that it would receive a charter. The contrast in the treatment given to the New University of Ulster and Buckingham is thus stark. And at a time when the universities are to lose 18,000 well-established undergraduate places, the government will be committed to supporting a further 470 places. Academic policy is thus being made from a position of simple and blatant political bias. If a left-wing Labour government comes to power it will have a splendid model of political interference in education to follow.

All of these measures add up to changing policies by stealth. The policies on 'new blood', information technology and overseas students restored a fraction of the cuts made, but on the government's narrowly political terms. At the same time, the boundary of the binary system has been shifted.

The same strictures apply to the government's treatment of academic tenures. The authors have never shared the view of many academics that tenure is essential to academic freedom. Carefully elaborated conditions of service, however, are important to personal welfare. In 1975 one of the authors advocated changes in the tenure rules in schools and universities, arguing that it should come later in a career but that the onus of making the case for its removal should rest increasingly with the institution as its holder became older. That kind of arrangement would be reasonable only when there were a decent market for academic labour, so that the less gifted and less well motivated would be able to move on to less demanding work. The general conditions of service would have to be changed if tenure were to be destroyed, in order to compensate for the loss of security.

But the arguments against tenure do not justify the way in which government chose to attack it. Had it allowed higher education to be cut back over a longer period, many institutions could have allowed older teachers to slip away and the issue would not have arisen in so acute a form. But it seemed to have no regard to its moral obligation to ensure that publicly funded institutions did not destroy the conditions of work on which people were recruited, and which implicitly affected other conditions of work such as salary levels. Moreover, for a government devoted to 'businesslike' methods, it was incredibly rash to have proceeded on this path without costing out the whole exercise. Moreover, it kept the universities waiting far too long while it made up its mind on how much to pay out in compensation. A further effect of both the cuts and the weakening of tenure and other conditions of service will be a sharp increase in the number of untenured staff on short-term contracts. This trend to 'proletarianisation', already evident before 1979, has been much accentuated.

The whole episode also serves to demonstrate the government's lack of faith in public institutions. This is at variance with the broader Conservative tradition that society must cohere through its public institutions. The Thatcher government did not believe in the power of public institutions to hold society together. It believed instead in the power of the market to advance the economy and to provide the incentives needed to keep people productive, happy and controlled. Because it did not care about the health of social institutions which assisted the personal development of individuals, it found it easy to insist on cuts which disarmed and humiliated higher education.

The government was wilfully destructive, and some academics accomplices after the fact. Although most higher education academics had become committed, in spite of earlier reservations, to an expanded system, some of those at the head of institutions and departments had only submerged earlier doubts, and those reasserted themselves once a government had the courage to force the issue. They disliked reductions because they took away resources, and resented the speed with which the cuts were imposed. Yet, pushed hard enough, many vice-chancellors and many of the leading academics in Oxford, Cambridge, London and the powerful civic universities, believed that the universities would do better if they shed some of their student numbers into the nether world of the public sector institutions. These sentiments constitute a perhaps unconscious betrayal of trust.

Our belief in higher education is simple and old-fashioned. Two potentially conflicting values ought to be present in the make-up of higher education's leaders. First, they should insist on high standards of work and ensure that their institutions are ruthless in eradicating irrationality, poor evidence and bad style. Second, however, it is intrinsic to the academic enterprise that academics respect not only the areas of experience of which they are masters, but also those of which they have little or no knowledge. The sociologist should be devout in defending the right of the classicist to advance knowledge of the ancient world. So, too, should the most deeply theoretical of scientists recognise the importance of applied work. Higher education should at once allow the pure scientist to reflect on the nature of the universe and train people to look after the sick and the old, or to put up bridges, or to collect tax effectively. And in such a scheme of things, the relationship would not be patronising, but would accept that creative work is often to be found in the messier parts of the intellectual labyrinth.

The strongest academics did not care enough for the fate of the weaker ones, even though they must have known that those who teach in the more privileged institutions are often very similar in terms of ability to those who work in a polytechnic or in one of the less prestigious universities. The sense of co-operation between academics has been ruptured, because the academics co-opted by government to allocate resources proved themselves too willing to do what was asked of them and not keen enough to stand up for higher education in general.

The government's policy damaged the universities by reducing their research capacity. It forced them to shed courses for which there was student demand. It damaged their sense of self-confidence and independence. It did so ostensibly to save money and then, under the stress of criticism, began to express hopes that fruitful reconstruction of the higher education system would result from the process of cuts. The chaotic methods with which the policy was imposed have produced many unintended consequences. If it was intended to cut student numbers, and with it student aid, the policy has failed: many more students have flooded into the public sector because the government failed to control it. If the government hoped that the universities would 'reconstruct' themselves under the pressure of cuts that, too, has proved to be a vain hope. Because the policy was imposed with no notice, and without regard to existing tenurial commitments, the universities could not reconstruct their academic plans in such a way that either their hopes for change, or the government's educational and social preferences, could be fulfilled. Instead, rightly from a moral point of view, they secured severances voluntarily and this meant that there could be little regard to the long-term planning of teaching and research.

The academic leadership of universities and public institutions was placed under enormous pressure. Vice-chancellors and directors have always had to balance their managerial and leadership functions with the need to preserve collegial ways of decision-making. Under the challenges set by the government, they inevitably tended towards managerialism. The problem of establishing good policies for universities emerged not only in individual institutions but also collectively. The CVCP has been criticised for being ineffective.[2] It has also been argued that the vice-chancellors are not the only members of universities who ought to formulate policies; members of university councils and senates and other leading staff should also be heard. Certainly, whatever the detailed solution, something needs to be done to strengthen both the legitimacy and the striking power of institutional policy-makers in the increasingly hostile environment set by government.

It remains to assess the extent to which the government's policy has affected access to higher education and whether it has saved money.

In Chapters 9 and 10 we showed that the universities had lost between 18,000 and 23,000 places for home and EEC undergraduate (according to the base year chosen) and over 5,000 places previously occupied by overseas students. There is no reason to believe that other ministers would have repudiated Rhodes Boyson's beliefs that fewer students should be recruited to higher education. Yet, as a result of the lack of control over the public sector, in 1982-83 and 1983-84 the number of students in higher education and the age participation rate actually increased, because of the enormous increases in the number of students in the public sector.

This unintended consequence of government policy will presumably be brought under control when the National Advisory Body begins to rationalise non-university higher education and ministers enforce more rigorous controls over local authority expenditure. But for the moment if they intended to cut the number of places they have failed. Whether government retrieves this failure or not, it will have demolished parts of the universities simply in order to let parallel courses in the public sector increase their numbers but on far less money than hitherto.

There is no official balance sheet of the savings produced by the cuts in higher education. We simply have an unexplained statement that the government expects to save 'at least' 10 per cent in real terms in spending by institutions between 1980-81 and 1984-85.[3] This figure may take account of some of the very large sums that the government has had to pump back to retrieve the results of its own actions. Against the large cuts in grants to universities and reductions in the local authority pool must be set many countervailing costs. First, the severance costs for universities, academic and non-academic staff, totalled £130 million. Equivalent figures for local authority staff are not available but the whole cost for both sectors and voluntary colleges may be as much as £200 million in one-off payments.

In addition to the cost of outright compensation there is the extra money universities will have to pay the superannuation funds to take account of the additional cost of meeting pension entitlements for those who, but for early retirement, would have remained in contributory employment. We have no figures for the other institutions, but taking the largest of the university schemes alone, which assumed that 3,000 of its members would retire early, the lump sum cost to be made up will be £85 million. A recent increase in employers' contributions included a 0.75 per cent element to meet this 'actuarial strain'.

Far from saving on student grants, the DES estimates have overshot by £35 million and £49 million in the last two years. Had student numbers come down instead of increased, however, the savings on public expenditures might simply have become a payment transferred to the unemployment and supplementary benefit claimed by young people at the end of the employment chain, whose jobs would be taken by their abler peers unable to find a place in higher education.

151

The government cut student places and money and insisted on cutting staff, but then replaced some of each of them by their own favoured schemes. New blood and information technology schemes will cost £100 million over three years. The restoration of help for overseas students, through Foreign Office aid, will cost £43 million a year.

Can ministers honestly say that they thought they would save only £120 million a year (ie about 10 per cent of the higher education bill) by these measures? These are marginal sums compared with other areas of public expenditure: for example, the Falklands policy is costing £400 million a year. And there are other costs which will not be paid in cash. There will be anger and frustration among young people, who are perfectly capable of understanding that 10 years ago their qualifications would have carried them into higher education. There will be anger, too, among higher education teachers and other staff who, having taken early retirement or been forced out of their jobs, will later reflect on the loss of status. The political backlash of drastically altering so many people's lives may not have to be considered but will eventually be given political and social expression. Injustices done to minorities are more oppressive than injustices done to majorities.

We have been highly critical of the government's attack on higher education. It has not only treated higher education, and its student clients, badly, but has also missed an opportunity to make beneficial changes. The boundary between public sector and university education certainly needs changing, some would say demolishing. But major changes have been made casually and without forethought. New positions have been established which the National Advisory Body, when it begins its task, will find difficult to change. The status of higher education teachers within the employment system could also have been subjected to rational and dispassionate consideration, which would have taken account of the special nature of their work, the privileges which they enjoy, and the balance to be struck between individual freedom and enjoyment of security and the needs of society. But that discussion cannot begin fruitfully under duress, and the certain result of government policy will be to discourage able people from joining the academic profession rather than to make sure that its conditions of work meet current needs.

Whatever policies are adopted, we argue that higher educational policy is a matter for public concern which deserves to be analysed and publicly discussed before major decisions are made. Simply to damage a set of institutions, and the people working within them, as part of a spasm of public expenditure cuts is neither efficient nor moral government.

References

1. *THES*, 6 May 1983
2. R Butler, 'The control and management of higher education in Great Britain, with special reference to the role of the University Grants Committee and the Committee of Vice-Chancellors and Principals', *Oxford Review of Education*, Vol 8, No 3, 1982
3. The Government's Expenditure Plans 1982-83 to 1984-85, Cmnd 8494 – II, Vol II, p 40, HMSO 1982

Index

privatisation, 140-1
and SSRC, 118-19
Committee of Vice-Chancellors
and Principals (CVCP)
criticism of, 150
and cuts, 32, 116-17
and tenure, 84-5
Community Enterprise Programme
(CEP), 143
Comptroller and Auditor General,
20
Computer science courses, 51
Conservative Party
government policy
1963 Robbins Report, 18-19,
20, 90
1972 White Paper, 16, 22-3
1979-81, 31-4, 37-40
1981, 11-12, 25, 88-92
manifestoes, 1979, 29
1983, 123-4
Council for National Academic
Awards (CNAA), 21, 26, 100,
131, 137
Courses
comparisons among, 66-7, 95,
96, 103, 106, 117-20, 123,
127-8, 145, 146
costs, 115
students, distribution, 62-5, 66,
91
UGC and, 51-2, 97-9
Cox, C B, 20
Crosland, Anthony, 19, 21, 22
Cuts *see* Expenditure White
Papers, Students, Universities,
University Grants Commission

Dahrendorff, Ralf, 33
Dankwerts, Peter, 114-15
Department of Education and
Science (DES)
and cuts, 1981, 88-92
estimates, 1981-82, 151
supplementary, 91
and polytechnics, 130-1
Department of Health and Social
Security, 106
DES Bulletin, 137

Douglas Home, Sir Alec, 18
Dundee University, 60
Dyson, A, 20

East Anglia, University of, 66
Eccles, David, 18
Economic and Social Research
Council (formerly SSRC), 119
The Economist, 140
Edinburgh University, 60
Education Act, 1944, 15, 18, 31
Education Act, 1980, 128-9
*Education: A Framework for
Expansion* (1972), 18, 22-3, 25,
39, 136-7
*Education after 18: Expansion with
Change*, 123
Education, Science and Arts Select
Committee, 55, 123
Edwards, E G, 36
Elton, Geoffrey, 113-14
Engineering courses, 95, 98, 115
Essex University, 66
Expenditure limits, LEAs, 128-9
Expenditure White Papers
1976, 27
1979, 32-3
1981, 34, 37, 42, 46-8, 68-71, 85,
89, 91
1982-83, 129, 130

Falklands policy costs, 152
Finance *see* Courses, Expenditure
White Papers, Students,
UGC, Universities
Flowers, Brian, Lord, 69, 110
Foreign Office *and* overseas
students, 36, 145, 152
Friedman, Milton, 31
*Funding and Organisation of
Courses in Higher Education*, 34

Government policy *see*
Conservative Party, Labour
Party
Grampian Health Board, 75
Grants
research *see* Research funding
students, 130-1, 136